Carmen's Legacy

Carmen's Legacy

By

John Maher

First published by Carmen Road Safety 2022

Second edition

PO Box 1315, Bakery Hill, Victoria, 3354 Australia

Copyright © John Maher, 2022

All rights are reserved except as permitted under the *Australian Copyright Act 1968*, for example, fair dealing for the purposes of study, research, criticism, or review. No part of this book may be reproduced, stored in a retrieval system, or transmitted in any form or by any means without prior written permission from the publisher.

For further information, see carmen.com.au.

Cover images courtesy of Bendigo Advertiser

Editing by Mandy Del Vecchio and Karen Guest

John Maher, Carmen's Legacy

Valuable chapters contributed by our children Michelle Trigg, Katrina Martin, and Jasmine Filmer.

ISBN print 978-0-6453890-1-2

Responses to Carmen's Road Safety Message

Past student
I graduated from high school a couple of years ago, and you shared Carmen's story with us. My friends and I always remind each other of Carmen when we feel a bit tired before driving. Her name comes up all the time, and although we didn't have the privilege of knowing her, we all feel connected to her story, which has profoundly impacted our lives. I always keep Carmen's bookmark in my car.

Student
I'd just like to say thank you, you presented Carmen's message to a group of my peers at our college. Many of my friends' bad driving habits were broken almost instantaneously after your presentation. I honestly believe, were it not for your presentation, some of them may not be by my side today.

Teacher
It has been three days since your presentation, and it has not left my mind. I've been teaching for 40 years and have heard countless presentations from professional circuit speakers to teaching professionals and so-called celebrities. Yours was by far the best I have ever witnessed. I cried a thousand silent and a few visible tears.

In memory of Carmen

Dedication

Life does not always hand out red roses.
This book is dedicated to:

Every brave parent who has lost a child in a car crash.
Every brave child who has lost a parent in a car crash.
Every brave child who has lost a brother or sister in a car crash.
Every brave grandparent who has lost a grandchild in a car crash.
Every brave grandchild who has lost a grandparent in a car crash.
Every brave partner who has lost their true love in a car crash.
Every brave friend who has lost a friend in a car crash.

Contents

Foreword 1
Preface 5
Part 1 You never know what's around the corner 9
    Chapter 1   How quickly life changes 11
    Chapter 2   I'm alive, but it hurts like hell 17
    Chapter 3   Our new life begins 29
Part 2 The day our hearts were broken, our lives forever
changed 41
    Chapter 4   18 November 1995 43
    Chapter 5   Our first days without Carmen 59
    Chapter 6   The day we said goodbye 67
    Chapter 7   Suddenly a family of five How do we cope? 73
Part 3 Looking back to look forward 81
    Chapter 8   Michelle's memories 83
    Chapter 9   Carmen's tree 99
    Chapter 10   Carmen's Racing Syndicate 103
    Chapter 11   Ten years 109
    Chapter 12   Twenty years 113
Part 4 Carmen's Legacy 115
    Chapter 13   Carmen changing lives 117
    Chapter 14   Supporting Carmen's Road Safety Message 125
    Chapter 15   Dad's a legend 131
    Chapter 16   Carmen's life lessons 137
    Chapter 17   Those left behind are the true casualties 141
Epilogue Our Lives Today 143
Acknowledgements 149
About the author 151
Facebook comments from students and schools 153
Connect with John 157

Foreword

By Mandy Del Vecchio

Carmen was *all-in*, all the time. There was no difference between smashing out a *Metallica* song on the piano, playing a competitive game of tennis, spending time with her horses, stringing together some ridiculous dance choreography, or telling a wicked story. She never did anything without enthusiasm. Her lust for life was incredibly grand.

In friendship, she was the same, *all-in*, all the time. Carmen's friendship would make you feel like a celebrity. She was a rare gem. You only realise how rare as you get older, as not all your friends are brilliant.

It was never hard to talk to Carmen. She was subtly generous in conversation, getting right behind anything you threw at her. A refined skill in adults and a beautiful, kind trait for a teenager.

She was big—and made big movements—all the time. Although delicately small in stature, when Carmen entered a room, it was an event. Ninety-nine per cent of the time, happiness drove her wild waves, although you would know if she was upset, and not often enough to even remember. She was also hilarious and could bring on whole-body-shaking laughs. I loved her so much.

On the morning of 18 November 1995, I woke early, hungover, and joyous after my year 12 formal celebrations the previous night. Around 8:30 am, the telephone on the wall started screaming through the peaceful morning. I dragged myself out of my crusty teenage cocoon to answer it. It was Carmen's sister Jasmine. She sounded like she was giggling so much she couldn't speak, and then she handed the telephone to someone else. I remember thinking it was fun they were up as well—I couldn't wait to share my night with Carmen.

'Mandy, Carmen's dead.'

I don't even remember who said that. The voice and the telephone were no longer present in my thoughts. I was suddenly alone inside my own silent scream.

Everything stopped. All sound escaped the room and my mind.

I dropped to the ground. My whole body shook, and I couldn't feel a thing. It was like the wonderful world so carefree minutes earlier had literally caved in below my feet, leaving a black hole for me to float in.

Losing a friend like Carmen was devastating. I was lost at such a young age.

We were 18 when Carmen died. I was a few weeks into *adulthood*, and Carmen a few months. It also meant she had been driving for a few months before me.

Carmen paved the way for our friendship group when it came to driving—and she was a great driver. As soon as Carmen got her probationary licence, she got her own car and claimed instant independence. It was enviable.

I got my probationary licence a few days before Carmen died. I had only driven a few times, and I remember I borrowed Mum's car twice that week to go to the shop for snacks.

I didn't drive again for about a year.

Carmen's death shaped me. Almost certainly, the strongest way it shaped me was as a driver.

The thing is, when you know the ultimate price for *little driving mistakes* so early on, you don't dare take any risks. Every risk meant death. It's something you can never forget.

What a heavy burden for a young driver.

Having Carmen's story with me saved my life many times over. I know it. I was a risk-taking teenager before that day and knew no consequences. I didn't think, and I did what I wanted. There is no doubt in my mind that I would have done the same with driving.

Having Carmen's story with me also saved the lives of my boyfriends, friends, colleagues and most importantly, my younger sister. I never let a friend take a risk when driving in a car. I spoke up when I saw the speedo flicker, or if I knew they had an extra drink, weren't concentrating, or hadn't slept enough. When you know the price, you must speak up.

I could have looked at Carmen's death as a burden on my driving, but instead, I know it was a gift. That's the way you turn tragedy into survival.

Carmen's dad, John, has given that gift to many teenagers and their families. His presentations are raw, real, and hard to listen to, but they are well-received. I know because, in 2011, I remember a colleague telling me how her 15-year-old daughter had come home from school, moved by a story she heard about a girl called Carmen. John had been at her school. My colleague talked about her discussion with her daughter after hearing John's presentation—Carmen's story—about driving, death, and devastation. Her daughter was shaped by Carmen's story and the conversation with her mum—as I had been.

John is selflessly giving this gift to as many teenagers as possible. As hard as it is to re-live Carmen's story over and over, he knows that once these teenagers have this story, they can't let it go. Like myself and my friends, we will all think twice before taking risks with our driving.

Thanks to my beautiful friend, Carmen, we are all safer drivers. That is her legacy.

Preface

At age 42, I was involved in a car crash that tragically took the life of an 18-year-old girl and threw my life and my family's lives into utter chaos. My injuries were significant, and they would change my life forever. Thankfully, I was not at fault in the car crash.

This was just the beginning of a horrific series of events for my family. Thirty months later, Carmen, our sweet, generous, hilarious, and vivacious youngest daughter, fell asleep at the wheel of her car. She hit a tree and died instantly. Carmen was 18 years and three months.

These two heartbreakingly tragic events could have torn our family apart. Instead, we became stronger together. As for me, I found my strength and purpose in life. With our lives shattered and wanting to make sense of what happened to our family, Carmen's tragic death gave me the power to change the lives of others. In the wake of losing our beautiful youngest daughter in a car crash, I embarked on a road safety campaign that has since impacted and, I believe, saved the lives of thousands of people over the past 24 years.

My purpose is to share my family's story, Carmen's story. I hope it spares at least one other family from having to experience our devastation. In doing so, the life or lives I might save are Carmen's Legacy.

To the best of my ability, this book recounts the happenings that shaped my journey, my family's journey, and, most importantly, honours our beautiful daughter, Carmen. It also highlights that even in your darkest hour, you can triumph over any tragedy with the love and support of family.

Ange and I are so proud of our girls, and I am honoured that Michelle, Katrina, and Jasmine saw fit to contribute a chapter each to our journey. This book describes Carmen's legacy.

Why is this book important for you and your family?

Unfortunately, our family is not unique. What happened to us has happened to many families. Sadly, it will happen to many more in the future. I hope that Carmen's Legacy can play a part in reducing those numbers significantly.

I don't claim to know everything, but I did experience the greatest loss when I lost my daughter to an avoidable car crash. Because of that, my presentations deliver a message that is hard to sit through but it's so empowering.

This book carries a meaningful message from my family to yours — you are the most important person in the world.

My story documents the strength of our family bond. It graphically recounts our steps as we worked together towards surviving Carmen's tragic death as individuals and as a family.

If this book can help one other family survive or, better yet, avert tragedy, my purpose has been met.

You are the most important person in the world.

A personal road safety message from me to you

You cannot do to your family what Carmen has done to ours.
You cannot die in a car crash because your family will never be the same, and they will never recover because you will always be missing.
Learn from our loss of Carmen.
Learn from my experience and stay safe for your loved ones.
Tell the people you love that you love them.
Tell them every day.
Cuddle your children every day, and then cuddle them again.
Because you never know what's around the corner.
I miss Carmen's cuddles.

John

Part 1

You never know what's around the corner

Chapter 1

How quickly life changes

In 1993 our family lived an idyllic country life on a beautiful 17-hectare property 20 kilometres from Bendigo in central Victoria. I had the job of my dreams as branch manager of a large life insurance company. My wife, Ange, stayed at home caring for our daughters. Our eldest, Michelle, was an apprentice hairdresser, and our three younger daughters, Katrina, Jasmine, and Carmen, attended Catholic College, Bendigo. We were all involved in sports, had strong community ties, and had a wide range of close friends. Life was perfect.

That all changed on Sunday 4 April.

It was a beautiful morning as Ange left for church in Axedale. I didn't join her because I had a cricket celebration to attend. The team I coached had won the premiership, and the team, supporters, and family members were going to celebrate the win with a barbeque at Axe Creek. Thirty minutes after Ange left, I borrowed Michelle's car and left for the barbeque.

Driving into Axedale, I slowed to 80 kilometres per hour, then slowed further as I prepared to enter the 60-kilometre per hour zone. I noticed a four-wheel-drive coming towards me, leaving the 60-kilometre per hour zone. Suddenly, it swerved across the road in front of my car. I slammed on the brakes and came to a complete stop on the highway. The out-of-control four-wheel-drive raced across the road in front of me. It looked as if it would crash into the trees on my side of the road, but then it swerved back towards me.

Shit.

I gripped the steering wheel and braced myself for impact. The driver of the four-wheel-drive had over-corrected. I watched in horror as the bull-bar on the front of the vehicle dug into the road, causing it to catapult end-on-end. It bounced so high into the air above me that I lost sight of it above the roofline of my car. And suddenly, everything went black.

It's black.
It's so black and peaceful.
The blackness just seems to go on and on.
It's the deepest blackness
I've ever seen, felt, or experienced.
The blackness embraces me
and feels like it is surrounding me,
holding me and comforting me.
I don't feel anything except the tranquillity
and the peacefulness of this
amazing blackness enveloping me.

A distant voice pierced the serenity.

'I can't see anyone, but whoever is in there has to be dead!'

It took me a few seconds to adjust and the words to get to my consciousness. Then the reality of the situation and what happened came flooding back.

And then those grave words jolted me out of my blackness, the blackness where I had found my peace and comfort.

'Hey, I'm ok in here.'

My response was feeble but urgent.

And then ...

The blackness again.

'John, can you hear me? Are you alright?'

This time, I recognised the voice. It was Ange, and she was calling to me from somewhere outside the car; the car I realised I was now trapped inside.

'Yes, I'm all right. I've got a broken foot, a broken nose, and a broken jaw ...' and even in such a dire situation, my typical humour kicked in when I added, 'but my dick's ok.'

And again …

Black.
The blackness has become my relief
from the incredible pain, the pain
I'm feeling throughout my entire body.

Consciousness returned, and the reality of my car crash really hit me. Visions came flooding back of my drive into Axedale—a four-wheel-drive vehicle losing control, a moment of fear, an impact, and the black.

In that small moment of consciousness, I tried to reach for the car keys to ensure the car was turned off. Such a simple task was impossible because I could hardly move.

Both front seats had broken on impact and collapsed onto the back seat. The roof of the car was now hard down on top of me. I was squashed by the roof into my seat, unable to see anything. I couldn't move my head, arms, or anything. I immediately had thoughts of the car catching fire. I knew if that happened, I was done for. I could also feel the car crushing my right foot over the brake pedal. The intensity of the pain in my foot and face was incredible.

The blackness saves me from reality again.

Until I heard another voice; it was much closer to me this time. 'Mate, can you hear me?'

It was a paramedic. He had somehow managed to crawl inside the vehicle and was now in the back of my squashed, wrecked car. 'Can you hear me?'

'Yes.'

'Do you know what's happened?'

'I've been in a car accident.'

'Do you know what day it is?'

'Sunday.'

'Do you know what time it is?'

'Just after 12 noon.'

'Do you know what the date is?'

'April 4, I think.'

'Well, I'll be stuffed. I can't believe it, I think you're alright.'

And I must have passed out again because the next thing I knew, he was saying, 'Can you hear me? Can you hear me?'

'Yes.'

'Can you reach back with your left arm because I need to put a drip in.'

All I could manage was to rotate my arm slightly. Thankfully, that was enough for him to insert the drip.

Black.

I woke again.

'How are the people in the other car?' I asked.

The paramedic hesitated before speaking the words that would haunt me for years to come.

'The young lady is deceased.'

I felt sick. My heart sank, and everything got heavy around me again.

Thankfully, I was overcome again by the blackness. It was a blackness that had become my friend and a place of refuge in all the pain and turmoil.

Another voice came from outside the car.

'Hang in there, John. You're going to be alright.'

It was my mate, Peter Elvey, who lived just 200 metres from the accident scene.

'They're just about to use the jaws of life to get you out.'

'Ok, Pete.'

Back to black.

When I next awoke, there was a lot of noise, grinding and crunching. And the pain was insufferable. I had pain in my face, back, and foot. The grinding was impossible to block out. It was horrific and all around me. It sounded like my mind felt. I wanted to scream through it.

More blackness.

The sound of an enormous crash woke me with a fright. 'Bloody hell, what was that?'

'It's all right. An oxygen bottle just fell over. We're in an ambulance and on our way to the hospital,' said Ange reassuringly, sitting beside me.

Thank heavens, I thought.

Blackness and peace.

The next time I woke, I was in the Bendigo Base Hospital emergency department and finally felt safe. I had never felt so out of control of my personal situation as I did while trapped inside that car.

I was drifting in and out of consciousness and being woken up by doctors and nurses. I was in enormous pain but thankful to still be alive.

Now that I was safe, my mind started racing. I couldn't shake the thought that a girl had died.

God, this is shocking, the poor girl.
What about her family, her poor family?
I wonder how old she was and who she was.

Ange was with me, and she was so calm. She didn't seem worried and kept telling me I'd be alright. I didn't feel like I was going to be alright. I felt like shit.

Ange told me Lesley Elvey was staying with our girls. Lesley was Ange's best friend, and she and her husband Peter stayed with Ange throughout the ordeal while I was trapped in the car. I was now thinking about our girls and how frightened they would be. Nothing like this had ever happened in our family. How horrible.

Doctors and nurses came in and out of the cubicle, taking my blood pressure, cleaning me up, and generally watching over me. I kept going to sleep—for how long each time, I don't know—but the doctors would wake me and check me out regularly. Ange never left my side, thankfully.

My top jaw was broken, and my cheekbones shattered. Doctors intermittently stuck their fingers in my mouth and invited others to do the same. The injuries were felt by pressing their fingers against the roof of my mouth. It hurt like hell.

The rest was a bit of a blur, but Ange kept filling me in. According to her reports, I already had an x-ray and a CT scan of my skull. I was being prepared to go to Melbourne for an urgent operation to repair my shattered face. A helicopter had been dispatched from Melbourne to pick me up.

I don't care, I thought, the sooner, the better, I just want to be fixed up, and I want the pain to stop.

Poor Ange. It must have been tough for her to be by my side and to see everything happening. It was ok for me because I kept dozing off.

I woke from another snooze to be told by Ange that they had turned the helicopter around, and I wouldn't be going to Melbourne after all. Fortunately, the doctor on call was trained in a new operating technique for my specific facial injuries. Ange agreed he should do the operation here in Bendigo. She knew I'd be spending quite some time in the hospital, so being able to stay in Bendigo would make it much easier for everyone.

Mum and Dad arrived from Bungaree, the small country town where I grew up. I don't remember much of what we spoke about, I was so tired, and I'd just about had enough of everything. I just wanted to be operated on and left alone.

Two more doctors were coming in to stick their fingers in my mouth. They were feeling the broken jaw and all the cheekbone pieces. It was like a deranged sport. I could hear my bones crunching and grinding as they moved their fingers around the roof of my mouth. They appeared to be enjoying the experience. To them, it was a curious injury. For me, it was a nightmare. The pain was absolutely excruciating.

Ange told me that I would be operated on immediately and she would see me when I got back. Thank God I was so ready for it. As I was wheeled into surgery, my thoughts were filled with my family and how fortunate my life had been up to that point.

This was never supposed to happen to our family or me.

Chapter 2

I'm alive, but it hurts like hell

I woke up in the recovery ward, unaware of what lay ahead. All I knew at that point was that I'd been in a fatal car crash that had taken the life of a young girl, and I was in pain.

I realised my life was going to change from that point. But how drastically, I never could have imagined. Feelings of uncertainty took over. Questions like: What will my future hold? How will this affect my family, my health, and my job? The reality that our perfect life could be changed so dramatically in an instant by a car crash started to sink in.

I thought again about the girl who had died, and I thought about her family. I wondered who she was and how old she was. I was imagining what her mum and dad were going through. While I could not bring myself to think about someone dying in a car crash I had just been in, it haunted my thoughts. My mind was flitting from the young girl who died to her parents, my girls, Ange, my mum and dad, to my work, and back through all of them again. It was a very disturbing thought loop.

Apparently, I spent some time in recovery before I was wheeled into a room that I would share with three other patients. As I was lifted and lowered onto my bed, the movement exposed how stiff and sore I was. Everywhere. The pain that started in my foot and face was now permeating my entire body. I couldn't get comfortable due to the constant ache in my back. I must have gone to sleep because the next thing I knew, I was being woken by a nurse. This was the beginning of what would become a ritual of having my blood pressure taken, lights shone into my eyes, and generally, having things done to me while attempting to sleep my way through the nightmare.

The next time I woke, Ange was sitting beside my bed. 'Am I going to make it?' I asked.

Ange assured me the doctor was happy with how I came through the operation and that I would be okay.

On day two, the ward was like Bourke Street, with people in and out all day. Dr Ian Poker was one of the visitors. He was the doctor who had operated on me the night before. Dr Poker arrived early to explain my surgery and injuries. He told me—in medical terms—that my top jaw had been broken in four places, two on each side. My cheekbones were shattered and collapsed—they'd been sitting inside and on top of the roof of my mouth.

During the operation, plates had been attached to each side of my jaw. My teeth had been badly loosened, so Dr Poker wired them together to give strength to my top jaw. This allowed him to rebuild my cheekbones by reattaching the bones with plates and screws and fixing them from my top jaw to my nose and eye sockets to hold everything in place. In all, I had 26 plates and screws inserted, and I looked beautiful again, apparently.

Dr Poker told me that because of the seriousness of the facial injuries and the rebuilding that had taken place inside my face, it was possible my bite may be out of alignment. He informed me if that were the case, he could fix it later with another operation where he would adjust the screws and plates.

There was a particularly nasty cut and gouge on my left upper arm, which I was told would also heal in time. My right foot had been x-rayed, and although it was not broken, it was badly bruised from being squashed over the brake pedal.

The doctors told me I'd be in hospital for quite some time, but they couldn't say how long until they saw how I recovered from the surgery.

Dr Poker seemed to be a good bloke, and he explained everything in terms I could understand. He also took the time to look closely at my injuries again and was confident I would make a full recovery. He was particularly pleased with how I looked after such a significant head trauma and a major operation. I had very little swelling considering the nature of the operation, and this pleased him. That he was so pleased gave me hope. When Dr Poker left, I felt at ease and believed I would be ok in time.

Later that day in the ward, when my curtain was pushed back, I introduced myself to my roommates. I announced, 'Hi guys, I'm John.'

'And you're bloody lucky to be with us,' was the immediate response from one of them.

'Yes, I had a car accident yesterday.'

'We know. It's the front page of the *Bendigo Advertiser*. Do you want to have a look?'

'No thanks.'

I was a little taken aback by the conversation, especially by how quickly the information about my crash spread and by how excited the person seemed to be that I was in his room and that my car crash was on the front page of the *Bendigo Advertiser*.

'An 18-year-old girl got killed in the crash,' he said.

'Yes.' I felt sick and uncomfortable with this conversation.

'How are you feeling?'

'I'm pretty sore, but I'm ok.'

'At least you're alive. It was a bad crash, going on this picture in the Addy.'

'Yes.'

'Do you know what happened?'

'I guess the young girl lost control,' I said.

'Well, at least you're here to tell the tale.'

'Yes, all I have to do is get better now.'

'You sure you don't want to look at the paper?'

'No thanks. I'm sure.'

'You've got plenty of bruising on your face and a couple of ripper black eyes.'

'Have I?'

I don't want to be part of this conversation anymore.

A reprieve. A nurse arrived to take my blood pressure and carry out the observations essential to assessing my progress. She was friendly and considerate and gave me something for the pain. I was thankful the conversation about the accident was over for now.

Shortly after, Ange arrived. It was good to see her and find out how our girls were coping. Ange assured me that, although they were worried, they were handling everything well. She also brought best wishes from my many friends who were thinking of us—wishing me all the best for a speedy recovery and extending their support to Ange.

Ange hadn't been with me for very long when someone came in with a huge bunch of flowers. He declared upon arrival, 'Hi, I'm Michael. I'm Emma's uncle. Emma's parents, Ian and Ann, asked me to bring you these flowers. They would also like to say how sorry they are for what has happened to you.'

Ange and I looked at each other and were confused about who Michael was. This must have been evident to Michael, as he went on to say, 'Emma was the young girl who died in the car crash you were also in.'

I was stunned and speechless. I couldn't speak for what felt like an eternity, but finally, I responded.

'Thank you, Michael. I am so sorry for what has happened. Can you please tell them how sorry I am?'

Immediately, I burst into tears. I couldn't help it. I was overcome by the gravity of the situation. Michael also became upset, and he soon left because it was an incredibly awkward and hopeless moment.

I couldn't believe that the parents who had just lost their daughter in a car crash could be thinking of me. They must be remarkable people to consider me at a time of such devastation and heartbreak for them.

Later that day, Ange brought our four beautiful girls in to see me. I was so happy to see them. I could have been killed in that horrific car crash and was lucky to see my girls again. I was so thankful. Ange told me the girls were frightened of losing me and, although they were looking forward to seeing me, they were anxious about what I might look like. I had 180 stitches—none on my face, thankfully—but it was bound to be a shock for them.

I learned later that when our girls first heard of my car crash, they feared they may lose their father. I can't imagine what that was like. In the beginning, they'd been at home for several hours with only each other as support and with only very brief and sketchy information about the crash. It must have been so frightening for them.

They could hear the sirens of the emergency services vehicles screaming up the highway, heading past our house to the crash scene just five kilometres up the road. They were horrified by how many they heard. Soon enough, they started getting phone calls from unsuspecting people saying they'd heard there was a huge crash out our way and asking if they knew anything about it. Not knowing what to say or how to say it, the girls said they didn't know anything.

Michelle was the first to speak. 'How are you feeling, Dad?'

'Considering what has just happened, I am pretty good. Sorry about your car, Michelle. How is it, do you know?'

'We're told it's a wreck, but I don't care because you're still here.'

'Yes, cars can be replaced, and at least it's insured.'

Katrina, our second eldest at 18, looked as though she had seen a ghost. Her concern at least allowed her to ask a question that was important to her.

'Are you in much pain?'

'Mainly my foot and back, but my face isn't too bad at all. So, how was school today?'

'It was ok, but we didn't really have our mind on our schoolwork with you in the hospital. Everyone was asking me how you were.'

'Well, now you can tell them I'm ok.'

Jasmine, 16, and Carmen, 15, were just standing there looking at me.

Carmen was hanging back a bit, and she was crying. They had probably imagined what I might have looked like, but it was still a shock to them. Each of our girls handed me a get-well card. As I read them, I could see the thought and love they had put into the words they wrote on each card. I could feel their pain and uncertainty as each card was so profound and vulnerable.

Carmen was just 15 years old at the time. Although Carmen's card was no more important than Michelle's, Katrina's, or Jasmine's, future circumstances elevated Carmen's poem to a level that impacted and empowered hundreds of thousands of people. I later reproduced Carmen's poem, 'Dad, I Love You', in the form of a bookmark, and it is repeated on the inside back cover of this book.

The whole experience was traumatic for us, and we had our own ways of dealing with it. It was tough. But at that very moment, while my girls stood around my hospital bed, I was happy. I thought of how lucky I was to have four fantastic daughters. I was very aware, as I am sure they were too, that I might have been killed. In times like these, you appreciate your family and what you have.

Ange and I did most of the talking because the girls were still a bit shell-shocked and probably needed time to adjust to seeing me in my state. After about 45 minutes of carefully worded conversation, I received my gentle hugs and kisses from my girls and Ange. They left for home with the promise to return at the same time the next day.

The next few hours passed by as they had before the visit. As I was continually monitored, I felt like a bystander in the centre of it all.

Nurses kept checking on me, and a few more bunches of flowers arrived. Being a nurse, Ange didn't appear to be fazed by my appearance or the pain I was experiencing. She was quite calm and just thankful that I was still there and in one piece. I was lucky I had two strong females in my life; Ange and my mum are both very nurturing and pragmatic, calm under pressure. You need people like them in moments like that.

My mum and dad were at our home supporting my family through this early period of uncertainty. Mum has always been good at reading a situation. I knew that Mum was taking the everyday family routine off Ange's plate so Ange could visit me and do the things that needed to be done.

Ange was my first visitor the next day, day three, and she was followed by a police officer from the Axedale Police Station. He asked me if I felt up to answering some questions relating to the accident.

He opened with the seemingly simple question, 'John, can you tell me what happened?'

I started to recount the events of the accident.

We established that my car had been stationary when the other car hit. He said that the impact of the collision had pushed my car eight metres back up the road towards Bendigo. I asked the officer the question that had been on my mind since the crash, 'Do you have any idea what might have happened to the young girl to cause her to lose control?'

The officer replied, 'Her name was Emma, and it appears that she got two wheels off the side of the road and into the gravel and then over-corrected.'

I burst into tears. I just couldn't help it. I simply couldn't stop crying.

Poor Emma.

I was thinking of the young girl being killed the moment our cars collided, and even though I knew it wasn't my fault, it was hard to take. My emotions took over. Unfortunately, my distress was such that the police officer called an end to the interview proceedings.

'Thanks for your help, John. That's enough for today. But we'll be in touch from time to time.'

The police officer left, and then I was out of control. I couldn't stop crying. I needed to know more about the young girl who had died, but I couldn't face it. Every time I thought of her, I became emotional and burst into tears.

Ange comforted me. The feelings were normal, she assured me. More flowers arrived. There were flowers everywhere. I was the only person in the room with flowers.

The pain was becoming unbearable. I felt I should tell a nurse, but I tried to put up with it. I didn't want to be a nuisance and felt I could suck it up. Thankfully, it wasn't long before a nurse came to take all my readings again, and I decided to ask for something for the pain. I got it immediately.

The braces on my teeth were bothering me because they felt bulky. But they saved me from losing all my teeth and supported the plates and screws that secured my cheekbones.

'So, how do I look?' I asked Ange.

'You've looked better, but you don't look too bad.'

'My right foot is killing me, and it does feel broken.'

'Well, the x-rays show no breaks in it.'

'Yes, I know that, but it feels broken.'

My assistant manager, Graham, and personal assistant, Bev, arrived with a huge bunch of flowers. They told me everyone from work sent their regards, and they were thinking of me. They also reassured me that everything was under control—and I didn't doubt that for one second.

'Vic Branch Office has been in touch and wants you to concentrate on getting better and not worry about work,' said Graham.

'Ok, that'll be easy, although, I must admit, I have been thinking about work.'

'Some people from Vic Branch will be up to see you in the next few days. You are to forget about work and just look after yourself,' was Graham's stern command.

As if on cue, another huge floral arrangement arrived from the Vic Branch. It was getting embarrassing as flowers were taking over the room. Ange decided to take some home with her. My work colleagues stayed for a while. I could see they were relieved to see I was doing okay, and they could take that message back to the office.

Night visiting hours were more suitable for many people as I had quite a few visitors in the evenings. I was happy to see Mum and

Dad, who dropped in often. They were relaxed and enjoyed spending time at our home, particularly with their grandchildren. I knew they would help to alleviate the girls' fear about our situation and my recovery. They'd be pleased to be 'doing their bit' to support us. It was good to have them with us, especially under these circumstances.

That night Peter and Lesley Elvey stopped by again. They were the friends who had been with Ange at the crash scene. Lesley had the most difficult job, supporting Ange while the paramedics, the SES, and the police worked to free me from the car. I can only imagine how anxious Ange must have been when they used the jaws of life to peel back the roof. No one had been able to see me while I was trapped in the car, so no doubt they had been very apprehensive about what state I would be in.

I was thankful to have Peter and Lesley there with Ange.

'How are you feeling?' asked Pete.

'Well, I have been better, but I'm not too bad, considering. I don't remember too much about what happened in the accident. How long was I trapped in the car for?'

'You were trapped for one hour and fifty minutes,' said Peter.

'Well, that's amazing. I can only remember about five minutes.'

'You know, that's probably a good thing,' said Lesley.

'I can remember talking to Ange, the paramedic, and you, Peter, but I don't remember anything else, not even getting out of the car.'

'The SES was amazing,' said Ange, with nods of approval from both Lesley and Peter.

At that moment, thoughts of the young girl in the accident came flooding back, and I broke down again.

'It's ok, you're all right,' said Ange.

'Yes, I'm ok.'

As I fought to stop the dark thoughts of the girl and the accident, I was glad the others didn't know what was making me cry.

Sensing he needed to break the mood, Peter opened a new discussion. 'I got everything out of Michelle's car before it was towed away.'

'I hadn't even thought of that. Good on you, and thanks. I guess Michelle would have had a fair bit of stuff in her car?'

'Really, there wasn't much. Anyway, I have it all,' said Peter.

'Thanks for being there for us and for looking after the girls. Boy, suddenly everything just happened, didn't it?' I said.

'Oh, that's all right, isn't that what friends are for?' said Lesley.

'We have everything under control at home, and the girls are coping well with everything since they saw first-hand that you're going to be ok,' said Ange.

'We'll be there to keep an eye on everything as well, and Ange knows that we are only a phone call away when Morn and Pop go home,' said Lesley.

Morn and Pop are my mum and dad, and although Pop is an easily explained grandparent name, Morn is unusual. Michelle, our eldest, christened my mum 'Morney' when she was learning to talk. Morney was her translation of 'morning,' which my mum would often say, in a singsong, as a greeting. Now everyone calls her Morney or Morn, and I must say it suits her perfectly for some reason.

The next day, Mum and Dad came in to visit me. I asked Mum if she was keeping the home fires burning for my return.

'Not in this hot weather, I'm not,' was her emphatic reply. 'You look much better than when we saw you in casualty. Much brighter and like your old self,' said Mum.

'Did you stay at casualty long?' I asked Mum.

'No, we just looked in to see you were going to be ok, and then we went out to be with the girls.'

Dad wasn't saying much, but that wasn't unusual for him. He was taking it all in and was relaxed about the whole situation. Still, I felt bad they'd been dragged into this drama, but because we are such a close family, I know they wouldn't have had it any other way.

On day four, I was surrounded by flowers and still in pain. The doctor came in, and after examining me, he said the stitches were ready to come out. As he removed all 180 of them, he commented, 'I'll stitch you up any time because I've never taken stitches out on the fourth day before. I bet you don't smoke.'

'No, I've never smoked and rarely drink.'

'That's fantastic. This is the proof of how a healthy body can heal itself.'

As soon as the doctor had finished with me, the physiotherapist was ready to work on my injuries. It was like a production line of things that had to be done. Dr Poker also came in to see me, so the physio had to stop for 20 minutes. Everyone was fantastic, and the nurses were brilliant, so my stay in the hospital was tolerable. Although I was in plenty of pain, I was well and truly on the mend with the help of everyone involved.

Early on the fifth morning, I awoke at 2:00 am and cried. I was thinking of Emma. I just couldn't stop crying. I must have cried myself back to sleep. This was to become a ritual at about the same time every night. I didn't even consider telling anyone about what was happening because I decided I could handle it myself. I believed that once I got home to my own bed, I would get on top of it, and it would be ok.

I would soon find out that this wasn't going to go away, and the tears would be a regular occurrence and a real problem for me. But I kept it to myself.

I felt vulnerable and uncertain, but there was hope.

Chapter 3

Our new life begins

At last, I was going home from the hospital. Ange picked me up, and as we drove home, I told Ange that I wanted to go straight to Axedale, where the accident had occurred. I'd been dreading the moment, but I knew that I had to face what had happened and to do that, I had to go back to the crash scene.

When we pulled up, I was already shaking. I guardedly stepped out of the car, and on my crutches, hobbled towards the crash site. There was a cross surrounded by flowers. Emma's name was on the cross. The tears came. I was crying and shaking uncontrollably. The trauma was rearing its head again. The thought of an 18-year-old girl being killed was crippling me. My heart was breaking for her and her mum and dad. The whole situation was incredibly distressing.

I could only cope with spending the shortest time there, just long enough to say a prayer for Emma. I had to leave; the memories of the crash and the thoughts of poor Emma were too much to bear.

Back home, I waited for our girls to come home from school and then for Michelle to come home from the hairdressing salon where she worked. When they were all home, we sat down to dinner, and at that very moment, I appreciated so much that we were all together as a family. Things could have been very different. After dinner, I sat in the chair, and Ange put the jug on. So began my new life. I was home and with my family again, but life had changed. The car crash wasn't just a car crash; it changed lives, so many lives. I now owned the crippling reality that my life would never be the same again. I started my road to recovery with a structured rehabilitation program, including physiotherapy and hydrotherapy three times a week. There were also multiple specialist appointments with four specialists that covered specific fields. I didn't realise how difficult walking and exercising injured muscles and tendons in a hydro-pool could be.

I had to accept the harsh reality that one day you can be running around playing cricket feeling fit and healthy. The next day you need to muster all your strength and courage to walk just five metres in a pool.

This strict program of hydrotherapy would continue for five months.

Working hard at my fitness was nothing new to me. I'd been a competitive sportsman, so I was prepared to do whatever it took to make a full recovery. Physiotherapy was challenging because I now had limited movement over much of my body. I found that using the crutches added to the pain I was experiencing in my back.

Although I was already under the care of four specialists, Ange had made an appointment with Dr Dennis O'Connor, our general practitioner (GP). When Dennis first saw me after the crash, he examined me thoroughly. He decided to see me every fortnight to monitor my progress. I had coached Dennis at Strathdale-Maristians Cricket Club, and we had a great relationship. I was pleased he would oversee my progress.

I was told to throw the crutches away three weeks after the crash. My foot supposedly had sufficient time to heal. I gave the crutches back to the hospital and—unsteadily and painfully—made my way without their support. My foot was still killing me, and it felt like it was broken.

After church the following Sunday, I stepped out of the car and stood on a small stone. The stone under my foot caused me to collapse to the ground in a heap. The pain was unbearable.

As I slowly got up, Ange asked if I was all right and exclaimed, 'You are as white as a sheet.'

My response was short and direct.

'My bloody foot is broken, and I don't care what they say. It's broken, and it's always been broken!'

The next day I went to see Dennis (my GP) and told him I had a broken foot and wanted it x-rayed again. He sent me for a scan rather than an x-ray, and that afternoon he telephoned me and said, 'I've got some good news and some bad news. Which do you want first?'

'I could do with some good news for a change. Could I have that first?'

'Okay, the good news is that you were right! The bad news is that the plate bone is broken underneath your foot.'

Given the nature of the break, they recommended it be screwed to repair the bone, but the specialist did give me an alternative. If I could continue to put up with the pain, I could just leave it, and it would eventually heal as it had already been healing for over a month. Choosing to leave it to heal itself over time wasn't a hard decision for me to make. The truth was, I couldn't bear the thought of heading back for another surgery, especially if it could be avoided. So, it can heal itself.

I developed a good relationship with Shane, my physiotherapist. When I was told my foot was broken, I immediately telephoned him.

Shane answered, 'Hi mate, what's up?'

'You bastard!' I exclaimed.

He was shocked.

I told him the initial x-rays showed my foot wasn't broken, and as he was the only one who had worked on it, it was obvious that he'd broken it!

There was a pause before his reply.

'I can fit you in this afternoon, so come in, and I'll break the other one for you.'

There is always a silver lining if you look for it, and over the years, Shane, who is still my physiotherapist, has also become a great friend.

Two months passed, and everything was starting to heal. I had now settled into the routine of seeing three specialists in Melbourne and one in Bendigo, plus my physiotherapy and hydrotherapy in Bendigo. Every part of my well-being was being accounted for.

I was in with my GP for a check-up one day when he asked, 'John, how are you coping with the fact that a young girl died in your car crash?'

I wasn't prepared for this question and immediately burst into tears and cried uncontrollably.

Apparently, not everything was healing.

'It's ok, you know it wasn't your fault,' said Dennis.

'It's not ok, Dennis. An 18-year-old girl is dead. She's dead, and it'll never be ok. I know it wasn't my fault, but she was the same age as Katrina, and she's dead.'

Thoughts of the young girl made it almost impossible for me to calm myself. Unfortunately, this was not unusual, but I was usually alone when I broke down. I had become used to these outbursts.

When I finally settled down, I told Dennis that I had been waking up crying every night since the accident but hadn't told anyone. He said he had been expecting something like this. Reaching into my file, he picked up Ivan Honey's business card, handed it to me and said, 'Ivan is a counsellor, and he's fantastic. He'll help you through this.'

Thank heavens Dennis asked me that question that day, as Ivan became an influential person on my road to recovery. I found that I couldn't talk about Emma at all without crying, which was embarrassing. Ivan said he could help me to cope with this but it would take time. Over the next few weeks, I discovered I had a myriad of other issues that were not being addressed. And, of course, everything was related.

One of the issues I was grappling with was trying to understand why I wasn't killed, and Emma was, yet my car had far more damage. This was a heavy burden for me to carry.

A funny thing happened after I'd been seeing Ivan for about three months. During a session, I brought up that practically everyone was asking me how I was recovering. This meant that many of my conversations these days were still about my car crash, which was draining.

We had a good session, and it finished right at lunchtime, so I suggested we have lunch together. About halfway through lunch, a woman came up to me and said, 'You're John Maher, aren't you?'

To which I replied, 'Yes.'

'I was one of the first cars on the scene after your crash, and it's a miracle you survived. It must be terrible to know that a young girl died.'

Ivan nearly fell off his chair, but it was the perfect example of what a walk down the street was like for me most days. These situations that kept cropping up meant that my car crash was always at the forefront of my mind. Discussing the crash so often made it difficult to move forward.

Another example of this was a week after I got out of the hospital when our parish priest, Father Marriott, asked if I would meet with the young woman in the car behind me at the time of the accident. She had some issues coping with what she'd witnessed that morning, so I agreed to meet with her. Father Marriott brought the young woman out to our home. When she saw me, she burst into tears. She couldn't control herself and repeated, 'You should be dead. You should be dead. You should be dead.'

It was confronting.

The visit might have helped her, but it certainly didn't help me.

I think Ivan began to better understand my plight after experiencing this type of encounter first-hand with me in the cafe that day.

I would go on to spend two years in counselling with Ivan. Although it was tough at times, Ivan helped me accept and learn to live with Emma's death, plus the impact of the many other crash-related issues that continued to impact my life. Without Ivan's guidance and support, I don't know how I would have coped.

The ongoing uncertainty was one of my biggest challenges. It felt like just as I was getting better in one area of my health, it would again worsen. I would take one step forward and two steps backward; if not in one area, it would be in another.

As problems would arise, the doctors would say to me, 'I was expecting that.'

I was beginning to feel like I should have a manual that could tell me what would happen next. That way, I could prepare myself as well as my doctors were. I hated the uncertainty.

I soon learned that I had a significant frontal lobe brain injury, and 26 plates and screws were inserted into my face to rebuild my top jaw and cheekbones. Ange made an appointment with Dennis to discuss her concerns about me becoming argumentative and forgetful. My family struggled with how forgetful I was and how aggressive I was in defending things when I was clearly at fault.

Dennis got the ball rolling, and soon one of my specialists referred me to a neurologist in Melbourne. She ran a series of tests and then requested another CT scan of my head. Only then was the magnitude of the frontal lobe damage detected and assessed properly. I was told the damage to the frontal lobe would cause me a variety of lifelong challenges.

During this period, when I was off work, it wasn't unusual for me to go into town to fill in my time, and often Ange would ask me to do some shopping for her. If it were just a few items, she wouldn't give me a list, and invariably, I'd end up coming home with not much of what she'd asked for. Sometimes I wouldn't do any shopping at all, and would swear black and blue that I hadn't been asked to do any. There were also occasions when I'd come home from somewhere, and wouldn't be able to tell Ange where I'd been because I had already forgotten.

Ange and the girls started to put sticky notes on the car's steering wheel, telling me what to do. I'd get angry with this and throw the note in the bin, and of course, I would then forget what I was supposed to do.

The forgetfulness would swallow up whole days sometimes, and it was like I was living in my own silent hell. On one particular day, I fell victim to my now unreliable memory and will never forget it. I went into town and was ready to return home again. The only problem was that I'd forgotten where I'd parked the car. I walked the streets for an hour before I decided to telephone Ange. I went to the phone box in the mall, but by this time, I was so flustered that I couldn't remember my home phone number.

A short time later, a work colleague saw me and said he wasn't surprised to see me in the mall because he had walked past my parked car. Relieved, I promptly asked him where he'd seen it, to which he replied it was in Queen Street. We had a short chat about my health and other stuff, and he went on his way. I was so overwrought by this time that I had no idea where Queen Street was, so I asked a woman on the street. She didn't know either, as she was a visitor to Bendigo.

Thankfully, I then ran into a friend, Kelly, and I thought I was finally saved. Kelly asked me how I was going, and I told her I was good. Trying to act as casual and composed as possible, I asked her where Queen Street was. She laughed, patted me on the shoulder, and said, 'Gee, you're a dag John, catch you later,' and then walked off.

This was now totally out of hand, and I was beside myself. In desperation, I walked up to another lady, and she pointed out that Queen Street was the next street. No wonder Kelly reacted the way she did. I set off limping, frustrated but relieved, and looking for my car on Queen Street.

I found it within half a block, with two—yes two—parking tickets on it. Annoyed, I got into the car and drove straight to the council offices and paid the parking tickets immediately because I needed this day and this chain of events out of my life forever. When I finally got home, Ange asked me if I'd had a good day in Bendigo. I told her I did.

I really didn't want to talk about my day.

Now that I was unable to work, I decided to pick Carmen up after school every day, which gave me something to do. I don't know how many times the school would telephone me at home at 4:30 pm, informing me that Carmen was still at school waiting for me. Carmen was amazing because she didn't worry or get upset with me for forgetting her. She'd tell me about her day or ask me about mine, trying to maintain as much normality as possible.

My short-term memory problems soon became the bane of my

existence. I found it difficult to accept that I had a brain injury. One of my great strengths in my previous life—the life before the car crash—was my memory, but now I was vulnerable, not to mention hard to live with.

I was forgetful, I was unreliable, and I was short-tempered. I wasn't handling any of it and was arguing with Ange and the girls due to my frustrations. It was four months since the car crash, and Ange worried I could have a complete breakdown. She was so concerned with my mental health that, after discussions with my GP, she organised for me to take a break and go on an interstate fishing trip with an old superules footy mate, Barrie.

The trip was just what I needed.

I flew to Adelaide, where Barrie picked me up from the airport, and we headed to his shack at Point Turton. The next day, we continued to Gleesons Landing, where the cray fishing camp was set up. I met some amazing people who accepted me with open arms, even though I was a Victorian. I was immediately named and introduced around as 'the Victorian bastard'.

The camp was set above a cliff, and although the view was fantastic, it was pretty rough, and with my health issues, there were some things I couldn't do. I had to be extra careful of my back.

This trip was my first time on the ocean, and just the experience of being part of the launching, by tractor, of a 26-foot boat off the beach into rough seas was a real thrill. Although apprehensive, I joined my new mates on deck as they pulled cray pots.

We weren't very far into the first day at sea when I realised I'd made a mistake. The way the boat bounced over the waves and slapped back down again really hurt my back, and I was in agony, but I couldn't say anything. After all, I was a Victorian. I didn't go back out on rough days, only when the seas were flat. I thoroughly enjoyed the two weeks I was there.

While on this trip, I was surprised to receive a message to make urgent contact with my state manager back in Victoria. I telephoned him from the phone box at Point Turton, and the conversation went something like this.

He said, 'John, there's been some changes made in the company, and under the new structure, there's no position for John Maher.'

My mind started racing as I struggled to comprehend what he was saying, replying, 'I beg your pardon. What are you talking about?'

He repeated, robotically, 'There's been some changes made in the company, and under the new structure, there's no position for John Maher.'

Then he hung the phone up in my ear. I walked back to Barrie, who was waiting in his car. I told Barrie I'd just been sacked. I was completely shattered. I couldn't believe that after all the years of service and loyalty, they could do something like that to my family and me, and over the phone of all things, and now, of all times.

We gathered up some more coins between us, so I could make my shocking phone call—I had to tell Ange what just happened. We cried over the phone, realising the enormity of the situation and what it meant for our future. Things were going from bad to worse, and I was not coping well with all the blows. Thank heavens my mate Barrie was there to support me when I was far from home. He was a rock.

When I returned home, there were more tears. Every time I looked at Ange, she would burst into tears. We both knew what this meant for our family—no job security, no income—and we were in real financial trouble.

Our saving grace was that I had income protection insurance. Unfortunately, though, it was nowhere near enough. I'd taken out the income protection six years earlier when I was 36, and at the time, I'd insured myself for 75% of the $75,000 I was earning. Remember, I was in the insurance industry but had never reviewed my income protection insurance. Six years after taking out the income protection, I was insured for just $50,000. I should have increased it to over $100,000 to account for my increased income at age 42.

Only two weeks before the phone call from the state manager that ended my job, two of the specialists in Melbourne had told me I would never work again. I had said to them, 'Rubbish, I don't believe you.' The possibility that my career was over was the farthest thing from my mind.

The state manager who made that phone call to tell me I no longer had a job was a great guy and someone I had greatly respected. We worked together for 16 years and had an excellent relationship. I ran into him in Melbourne about 18 months after that dreadful telephone call. He was on the other side of the road, so I crossed over to meet him. When he saw me coming, he put his hand to his forehead and said, 'John, I hoped I'd never run into you again after what I did to you.'

I invited him for coffee, and he accepted.

We sat and had coffee, and I asked him, 'Why did you hang up on me after you told me?'

'Because I was crying,' he replied.

I do not doubt that for a second. It would have been difficult for him to make that telephone call because he and the company respected me and had big plans for my working future. But my car crash changed all of that and brought my working life to a screaming halt. My short-term memory problems alone meant I could not provide financial advice or train people to give such advice again. It was the decision they had to make.

A car crash is not just a car crash.

Our lives settled down eventually, as we found a routine, and I began to accept what had happened. My 'forced retirement' days consisted of teaching myself to use a computer—I was a slow learner, but I persisted. I kept crashing the computer, and Lesley kept resurrecting it for me. I also loved walking in the paddocks, looking at my horses, and sitting by the dam. I often drove into town trying to fill in time between the doctor, physiotherapy, and counselling appointments, which were all now a part of my weekly routine.

I also developed some challenging health issues. One was this astounding stress rash that seemed to have a life of its own. Of course, it invaded my nether regions, and I felt like I was on fire. It was bright red like a neon sign that didn't turn off.

One hot summer's day after seeing my GP about the rash, I was home alone and couldn't bear to have my pants or jocks on any longer. So, I set up the fan beside the couch near the back door in the kitchen, pointed it at my nether regions, and enjoyed the cool air blowing onto the damn rash. I lay back in all my glory to watch TV and enjoy cooling everything down.

Things were working perfectly until there was a knock on the glass kitchen door. It was Matt, a neighbour, and in all the years in this house, no one had ever come to the back door. But here was Matt.

My bare nether regions were aimed squarely at the said glass door, and Matt got more than he had bargained for. I wasn't happy and never cooled myself there ever again. I think both Matt and I were scarred for life from that experience.

I wasn't sleeping well, and as a result, I became easily agitated. This put me even deeper into depression and was the worst place to be. I lost my appetite and weight, but I was not going to give up.

Due to the severe pain in my back, travelling in the car was difficult. I couldn't travel more than 30 minutes without stopping to walk around to ease the back pain. Over time I would stretch that out to 60 minutes, but it was still a damn nuisance.

Ange had gone back to work to help out financially because the cost of living had increased due to my injuries. There were costs for medication, doctors' appointments, and regular trips to Melbourne to see specialists. By this stage, we also had two children at university. Life wasn't easy.

My life, and even my family's, was now centred on facing my inability to do many things. Our schedules were governed mainly by the many appointments I was required to attend, all related to my car crash. The latest car crash-related commitment was with the solicitors who were now involved, which added to my stress levels.

Our lives had changed so much that we didn't know what challenges we might face in the immediate, medium, or long term. I kept myself occupied as best I could, and was hopeful that everything would continue to improve. It was a painfully slow process, but at least I was on the right track. Because of my injuries and their flow-on effect—medical, physical, and emotional—my family faced one of the biggest challenges we ever had to face: my recovery, all from that one damn car crash.

A car crash is not just a car crash.

Part 2

The day our hearts were broken, our lives forever changed

Chapter 4

18 November 1995

Some of the most beautiful mornings are remembered for the most horrific reasons.

It was Saturday 18 November, one of those beautiful spring mornings, one right out of the box—sun shining, crisp fresh air. I was up earlier than normal because we had plans to go into Bendigo to do fundraising.

Just 30 months after my car crash, my family was slowly rebuilding our lives and preserving ties with the community. We had found ways to give back to our community, to those less fortunate, which was a small part of the rebuilding. At least, it was for me. As a family, we were going to tin-shake in Bendigo on behalf of our eldest daughter Michelle. She had committed to raising funds for the then Spastic Society of Victoria (now Scope). Ange, Jasmine, Carmen, and I were excited about our Saturday adventure.

The morning played out like your average Saturday, I guess. At 8:15 am, I briefly chatted with Michelle, and then she left for work and gave us a toot as she drove out the gate.

Carmen left the house at 7:30 am to drive her best friend, Carmen Trevean, into town for work. Carmen stayed overnight as she had done hundreds of times before. The two Carmens had been best friends since primary school and were inseparable.

The girls were up before us that morning because Carmen Trevean worked part-time at McDonald's Bendigo. Despite having a late night talking in the bedroom, as teenagers do, Carmen was up early because she had to drive her friend to work as she didn't yet have her licence.

Three months earlier, Carmen got her licence on the first attempt, the day she turned 18. She was over the moon about it. She loved driving, loved her independence, and was a very good driver. I taught all my four girls to drive; they're all good drivers, but Carmen was very good and fully prepared for sitting her test. She loved her little car so much that she couldn't wait to get behind the wheel.

I hadn't seen the girls before they left, but with the 40-minute round trip into McDonald's, it wouldn't be long before Carmen would return home, so we patiently waited for her. We'd planned to leave home by 8:30 am to make the 20-minute trip to the fountain in the centre of Bendigo for our fundraising tin-shake.

I don't remember having breakfast, but I guess I did. I don't remember everyone rushing around to get ready, but I guess we did. I remember putting the fundraising collection tins and banners into the boot of the car. I remember it because it was then, when I was standing at the back of the car with Ange and Jasmine, that I heard a car coming up Hawkins Lane.

While standing in the driveway, my gaze shifted from the beautiful grey-green gum and colourful bottle-brush trees surrounding our driveway to flashes of white as a car travelled behind the trees and slowed before turning into our gate. It didn't look like Carmen's car.

I was surprised to see it was a police car. It wasn't unusual for people to call into our house and ask for directions to properties in the surrounding area, so I approached the police car to see if I could be of any assistance.

A young police officer stepped out of the car, and he was crying. I was confused, but I figured that something was wrong. At the same time, I noticed his tears; I saw someone sitting in the back of the police car. I couldn't make out who the person was because of the tinted windows and because my concentration was focused on the young officer.

'Good morning, can I help you?' I asked.

'There's been an accident,' the young police officer replied.

'What's that? There's been an accident? Where?'

'On the way into Bendigo. It's your daughter.'

I couldn't comprehend what he was trying to tell me. He continued, 'Your daughter has had an accident in her car.'

'Oh no! Is she all right? Is anyone hurt?'

'It's Carmen, and she's gone,' was the police officer's hesitant reply.

'She's gone? Gone where? What do you mean she's gone?' I struggled to come to grips with the conversation.

The police officer continued, clearly and routinely, 'Carmen has been involved in a car accident, and she's gone.'

I still couldn't work out what he meant. I became frustrated and alarmed and shouted, 'Mate, what are you talking about? Where's Carmen gone to?'

I could feel my blood pressure rising because there was something wrong here. I was so angry and so confused.

I assumed it was Carmen in the back of the police car and demanded, 'Carmen! Get out of the car. It's ok!'

The back door of the police car opened, but it wasn't Carmen. It was Michelle. As she stepped out, tears were streaming down her face, but I was thinking …

> *Michelle, it's ok, as long as you're all right.*

'Michelle, what's going on?'

Michelle held her hands out towards me and said the words none of us can ever forget, 'It's Carmen, Dad. Carmen's gone. Carmen's dead!'

> *My emotions exploded—*
> *confusion, shock, horror, and disbelief.*

The next few seconds unfolded in a blur. Jasmine collapsed to the ground, and Michelle rushed to her. Ange and I were hugging each other, and we were all crying. Everything was so confusing. I don't really know what happened next or in what order. It was too difficult to comprehend that Carmen could be dead.

Now we were all cuddling, including the young police officer. I tried to compose myself and bring the situation back to reality, so I asked the police officer where the accident had happened. He told me that it was near the Farmers Arms Hotel.

'I'm going there. It might not be Carmen,' I said.

I pulled myself away from the cuddling and crying and marched quickly towards my car.

Michelle screamed, 'Dad, don't go there, please don't go there, Dad!'

The young police officer intercepted me at my car. He stood in front of me with his hands clasped, praying, and said, 'Please, Mr Maher, don't go to the crash scene. Your family needs you here.'

I knew he was right. And at that moment, I made the worst decision of my life—I stayed with Ange, Michelle, and Jasmine. Because yes, they did need me, and we needed each other. But to this very day, I wish I had gone to Carmen. I should have gone to Carmen to be with her, to hold her hand. If there is anything that I could change in my entire life, it is that I would have gone to the accident site to be with Carmen. Instead, I left her there alone.

I sought out more facts in another attempt to bring some reality to the situation. When we were inside the house, I asked the police officer what had happened. He explained to us, calmly and methodically, that Carmen's car had left the road and hit a tree. A witness had seen Carmen with her head on her chest as the car drifted across the road in front of her before hitting the tree. Carmen may have fallen asleep, the police officer said. I asked him if anyone else was hurt, and he said no.

Carmen's car left the road and hit a tree.

The next few minutes played out like a scene in someone else's life. Ange sat on the couch, and the police officer stood beside the sink and made us a coffee. Michelle and Jasmine were both sitting at the kitchen table, holding each other. A thick, dark cloud encompassed the space all around us! I tried to sit but I couldn't; I wished I could be with Carmen. But I also knew that Ange, Michelle, and Jasmine needed me. I was not much good to anyone. I think I was totally useless.

Carmen's Legacy

*One moment it was a sunny morning,
and within minutes, it had become
the darkest day of our lives.*

I couldn't stop thinking about Carmen and myself, and Carmen and us, and I wondered how our family would cope with Carmen not being in our lives. Over and over, I was thinking:

*This can't be true.
This can't be happening.
Carmen can't be dead.*

As I paced the floor, anger built. And then I snapped, unleashing on the closest object, which just happened to be a footstool. I kicked that stool across the room and almost put it through the glass door. I realised I scared Ange and the girls and buried my head in my hands.

Other thoughts soon pushed their way into my head.

Oh God, what are we going to do?

And then,

Oh no, I have to call Katrina.

Our second eldest daughter, Katrina, was living and working in Sydney. At this stage, my inner voice began to spin out of control.

*How can I tell Katrina?
What about my mum and dad?
What about Ange's elderly mum?
My brothers and sister?
And what about Hughie and Sandra and their girls?
And what about Ange's sister Marie?*

It was already a shocking nightmare for us as a family, and now everyone would be pulled into this hell. The reality was that they must all be told, and we needed them to be with us because we needed their support. We all needed to be together.

One thought stayed fixed above all.

Poor little Carmen.

The time came, and I had to steel myself to make the first and most difficult call to Katrina, better known as Trin. She was 21 and had moved to Sydney for her career. Trin was the assistant manager of Australia's second-largest Betts & Betts shoe store. We were so proud of her and kept in contact almost daily, but I never imagined I would ever have to contact her for something so horrific.

I dialled the number. The phone rang a few times and was answered by one of Trin's colleagues. Firmly but anxiously, I asked to speak to the manager. I told the manager the dreadful news that I had to give Trin, and I asked if he could please be near our daughter to support her when I told her that Carmen was dead.

Trin came to the phone, and before I could say anything, she sang in her usual cheery voice, 'Dad, fancy you are calling me on a Saturday morning! I didn't even want to come to work today. You've made my day!'

> *How am I going to break this girl's heart right now?*
> *Now, when we can't be with her.*
> *Our little family has splintered.*
> *Trin is not with us,*
> *and Carmen is not with us — never again.*
> *Our poor Carmen.*

'Trin, I've got some really bad news to tell you. There's been a car accident, and I'm sorry, Trin, it's Carmen. And Trin, I'm so sorry, Carmen is dead.'

On the other end of the phone, I heard poor Trin saying, 'No Dad, no Dad, not Carmen Dad, NO DAD NO.' And then silence as Trin dropped the receiver.

I have thought about that phone call often, and there is no other way you can tell a daughter and a sister that news. There is no soft way of breaking it. How else do you tell your daughter over the phone that her sister has just been killed in a car crash?

Poor Trin. It must have been so hard and lonely for her to receive this shocking news. I knew we had to get Trin home as soon as possible.

Trin and I talked, and we cried, and I told her we would arrange a flight for her so she could come straight home and be with us as soon as possible. Trin wanted to keep talking because she needed support, even if it was just over the phone. We talked for a while, and it was tough to hang up on Trin when I knew how much she needed me, but I had to telephone Mum, Dad, and everyone else. If I had it my way, Trin would have been there with us then. But so too would Carmen. This was a disaster beyond comprehension.

A work colleague of Trin's drove her home. Her close friend and roommate met her at home and helped her pack a suitcase, which included an outfit for her little sister's funeral. Poor Trin then had to sit alone on a flight full of strangers from Sydney to Melbourne, trying to deal with this horrific news.

Poor Trin.
Poor Carmen.

I had to call Mum and Dad, but I rang my brother Brendan before I did. I told him what happened and asked him if he could go out to Mum's to make sure our parents were all right.

I dialled the number and Mum answered the phone. 'Hi Mum, is Dad there?'

Mum sensed something wasn't right because mums have that sixth sense.

'John, what's wrong?'

'I just need to talk to Dad.'

'John, you tell me what's wrong. NOW!'

'Mum, I have some terrible news. There's been a car accident, and I'm so sorry, Mum, it's Carmen. And Mum, Carmen is dead.'

I then heard my poor 68-year-old mum scream out to Dad. 'Jack, Jack, Jack, my God, Jack, Carmen's been killed in a car crash.'

Poor Mum and Dad.
Poor Carmen.

And the calls continued. I called all my brothers and my sister Carmel. Then I called Ange's family, including Ange's sister Marie, who lived in Maroochydore, Queensland.

The next phone call was to Ange's brother Hughie and his wife, Sandra, who lived in Myrniong. I gave them the unenviable but important task of booking Trin's flight back to Melbourne, meeting her at the airport, and bringing her home to us in Bendigo.

My next call was to Rhonda Trevean, Carmen Trevean's mum, who Carmen had dropped off at work just 60 minutes earlier. Carmen Trevean was the last person to see Carmen alive. This was a hard call, but I needed Rhonda to know her daughter was safe.

The phone rang only a few times, not long enough for me to prepare. My whole life had not been long enough to prepare for this.

'Hi Rhonda, Carmen dropped Carmen off at McDonald's this morning …'

'Yes. I know,' Rhonda replied, 'because I've already spoken to Carmen at work. Can you thank Carmen for dropping her off for me?'

'Rhonda, you'll have to go out to Carmen because I have some horrible news. Carmen's had a car crash on the way home, and Rhonda, I'm so sorry, but Carmen is dead.'

Poor Rhonda just started sobbing. Our Carmen was like a daughter to her, just as her Carmen was to us. We both knew this news was going to destroy her daughter. I thought of her, that poor girl. I thought how no one should have to lose their best friend so early in their life, especially in such a tragic way in a car crash.

Poor Carmen.

The next hour was a marathon of intense, sad, and heartbreaking calls. I opened the teledex, which contained the phone numbers of all my friends, plus Ange, Michelle, Katrina, Jasmine, and Carmen's friends. Between us, Ange and I telephoned every one of them. We made well over 160 phone calls. Dead phone calls.

I made about 15 or 20 phone calls and paused for a moment before making the next one when the phone rang. I answered it, and someone on the other end of the phone screamed, 'John, please tell me it's not true.'

This contextualised the entire process that continued throughout the afternoon as we made those dead phone calls to our friends. We answered all the calls that came in, many from people we hadn't heard from for years and years. Then it wasn't long before people started to arrive at our home. One by one, our home filled up with family and friends.

It was like the start of a big family get-together, a party, but the mood was despondent and unfamiliar. It was surreal. I remember that feeling so clearly, and even when thinking about Carmen's death today, I realise that feeling has never left me.

I just wished the whole thing wasn't happening. I wanted it to go away. I wanted to wake up and find that I had been embroiled in the worst nightmare of all time.

Thoughts continued to float through me.

Poor, poor Carmen.
I wonder what they are doing to her now.
Is she still trapped in the car?
Is she in the ambulance, or is she in the morgue?
What are her injuries? Did she suffer?
I should be with her.
I hope Katrina's ok.
Poor Trin.
Poor Carmen.

The house was full of guests. Loved ones were filling the empty spaces, attempting to mask the dark cloud that now resided in and over our home. Heavy-hearted, we received the next houseguests—Carmen Trevean and her parents.

Carmen's mum, Rhonda, was pale, crying, and apprehensive, while her dad, Mark, stood back, holding his emotions in. He always called our Carmen 'his other daughter'. Carmen was not able to hold anything back. The poor little thing was broken. We cuddled her. She was crying and trembling. In just a few hours, her world had turned upside down. Her best friend was gone, they had said goodbye in the little car, and that was the last goodbye she would ever say to her best friend. I envy Carmen, though, because she was the last person to ever see our beautiful Carmen.

'I'm sorry. I'm so sorry. I'm so sorry,' Carmen kept repeating. At 18, she had just lost her best friend in a car crash, and I knew she was feeling partly responsible at that moment. But she wasn't. It was out of her hands. And as we know, life will do to you what life is going to do. Life isn't always fair. None of us deserved this, and Carmen certainly didn't deserve this. My heart was breaking again.

> *How can all this be happening?*
> *This is just shit!*
> *Poor Carmen.*

My brothers and sister arrived with their families from Ballarat, then my mum and dad from Bungaree. Being such a close family meant we always supported each other. It seemed our closeness only magnified the pain for all of us. We were all there, as a family, ashen-faced, dumbfounded, and broken-hearted, for each other and for Carmen.

I looked at our girls, Carmen's sisters, cousins, and friends. The reality was apparent. Their lives had just been blown apart in an instant. They, like us, were never going to be the same. They would know true grief and tragedy every moment beyond this awful day. They would never lose that feeling, which is so unfair at such a young age.

Katrina finally arrived from Sydney to join the gathering of our family and friends. Poor Trin, I thought. This hurt was unrelenting, and while she was away from it, perhaps she still had the hope that it was all just a bad dream. But she was now in this cold hell with the rest of us. Ange's side of the family was now arriving.

The comfort I got from knowing my three girls were finally together to support each other was fleeting. I was shattered as I realised that up until that day, we had four beautiful girls— Michelle, Katrina, Jasmine, and Carmen. It was always our four girls.

And now, there were only three.

> *But it's always been 'and Carmen'.*
> *My girls have lost their little sister and their friend.*
> *Their lives will never be whole again,*
> *there will always be a huge void:*
> *a loss that can never be replaced, an ache.*
> *We will never be all together again, never!*
> *How will we ever heal?*

Carmen's Legacy

> *We can never again be a whole and happy family.*
> *And what of Ange and me?*
> *Well, we'll go on, we must.*
> *Because we still have three wonderful daughters.*
> *But we can never recover because we've lost Carmen.*

A procession of shocked, caring faces surrounded us. It extended their support, some coming, some going, but all of them with us because at eight minutes past eight that morning, our youngest daughter, Carmen, was killed in a car crash. Our lives had been shattered because Carmen was dead. Everything was becoming so overwhelmingly hopeless, and it was impossible to comprehend but even more impossible to accept.

> *Poor Carmen.*
> *Poor us.*

Our immediate families were all with us now, Michelle, Katrina, Jasmine, Carmen's grandparents, uncles, aunties, and cousins.

They had lost someone precious because everyone loved Carmen so much. She played such a huge part in all our lives, and she was so often the life of the party. Thank God we have all that video footage, I thought, and those fantastic photographs from our many Maher and Miller get-togethers, but I knew it would never be enough.

With flowers in every room and flowers lining the walls the entire length of the hallway, the florist's car still came to deliver more. People brought cakes, sandwiches, and biscuits. Everyone was so considerate. David and Mandy, Carmen's employers at the Eaglehawk Hot Bake, sent out an enormous amount of food in their van. And they just kept sending more. They had not just lost an employee like us; they had lost Carmen.

Our loved ones never left us alone that whole day. We talked, we cried, we smiled, we cried, we cuddled, and we cried some more. We uttered consoling words and were offered consoling words. It was hard to comprehend how long one day could last. It was everlasting. And the heartache didn't let up all day.

It felt like a strange reunion with all the people who came to pay their respects, some of whom we hadn't seen for years. However, a dark cloud engulfed everyone. It saturated everyone with sadness. There were no breaks in the cloud. No glimpses of sunshine at all. There was no escape from our collective tragedy. This sunny Saturday had become a dark day, devoid of hope.

At one point, I slipped away into the guest room to have a damn good cry, but Mum saw me and followed me in and caught me crying. I told Mum I'd only slipped away for a minute because I needed to. Mum told me that I had to be strong for Ange and our girls. I knew I had to be strong for them. But at that moment, I just wanted and needed to cry. For Carmen. Just for a minute. So, I cried.

I have cried so much for Carmen since that Saturday. Typing everything here like this, I've cried many more tears. But I don't mind because I love Carmen. I'm happy to cry for her whenever I need or want to.

It was almost time to end this dark, dark day. The sun had gone down hours earlier, and it was time for bed. But it didn't end there because when it was time to go to bed and finally close our eyes on this seemingly eternal day, things only got worse. I entered the most intense, heart-wrenching, lonely and hopeless moment of the day.

Ange and I were in bed together. We were now alone with our thoughts. My mind was racing, and my thoughts were out of control. And they were all about Carmen. I continued to spiral into a heavy drift as I tried to comprehend what made her crash the car.

Did she go through any pain?
What were her injuries?
Where was she now?
Was she on a cold slab in the morgue on her own?
How were they treating her body?
What are they doing with our Carmen?

I knew she was dead, but the thought of her on her own on a cold slab would not leave me. More thoughts flooded in.

When did I last tell Carmen that I loved her?

In my head, I told her ...

> *I love you so much, Carmen.*
> *Please don't let this be happening.*
> *Please don't leave us all like this.*

And then I thought of Ange, Michelle, Katrina, and Jasmine. I knew they were going through the same terrible emotions as they tried in vain to fall asleep—as if sleep could make all this go away for a little while. Maybe at least until the morning, I hoped. I couldn't say anything to Ange because nothing could help the situation. There were no words, and there was no hope. What were we going to do? I just lay beside Ange under this heavy cloud. The bed was shaking from Ange's crying, and it just wasn't fair.

Our house was full of guests. So many people stayed the night, and I knew they were all trying to sleep. I could feel the sleepless souls. We had uncles, aunties, and cousins sleeping on the floor, couches, chairs, and anywhere they might feel reasonably comfortable. No one could bear to go home and leave us alone with this. At this moment, everyone needed the support of each other because this was a disaster beyond comprehension.

My mind was still racing, this time through the 18 years and three months we spent with Carmen. So many memories. Memories that were just locked in my mind. She was now just a collection of memories. How was that fair?

HOW IS ANY OF THIS FAIR?

I thought of our three girls, their cousins, the Millers, and their four girls. An image of the girls from earlier in the day, distraught, came into my head. I thought of the 18 years our girls and the Miller girls had spent growing up together. Two groups of four sisters. The closest of cousins, their lives had always been so parallel. They had 18 years of happiness and playfulness as fun-loving cousins, and now everything was shattered. The loss of Carmen had shattered their happy and carefree lives.

> *We had four girls this morning.*
> *And now Carmen is dead.*
> *She's gone forever.*

This kept repeating in my head.

I didn't know how long I'd been in bed. I didn't know if Ange was asleep yet, although I was pretty sure she wasn't. For the time being, at least, she had stopped crying. I prayed to God so hard to let it be a terrible dream and let Carmen be tucked away in her bed in the morning. I just wanted everything to go back to normal. And then I realised, no, Ange wasn't asleep. She was crying again. The bed was shaking. It was all real.

I couldn't find anything positive to think about. Everything was closing in on me. I kept thinking I should have been with Carmen because she was alone, and I hadn't even said goodbye to her. I hadn't told her that we all love her so much and that we would always love her. I wanted to be with Carmen. I hated the thought that she was alone on a slab, and it would be so cold and clinical. Carmen's life had been so full of warmth and love, and where she was now had to be so lonely and cold, nothing like what she'd known all her life.

My.

Heart.

Was.

Shattering.

How can God do something like this
to someone so beautiful and loving?
How can the life of someone so young be taken?
Someone so full of life, fun-loving,
and just starting their life's journey.
How can God be so cruel to Carmen
when all she did was do kind
and caring things for so many people.
More to the point, why did God let me live
through my car crash
and then take Carmen like this?

I kept thinking it's just not fair. I was 42 years old when I had my crash, and Carmen was only 18. Why wasn't I taken instead? She was just starting her life journey, and God had taken her and left me. It wasn't right.

As I lay awake, I played out a conversation in my head that I'd had with Carmen only one month earlier. I asked Carmen how much money she had saved in her bank account, and she said $18. When I asked her what she was doing with her money, I found out that she was buying presents for her friends who were either still at school or were less fortunate than her. I explained the need to save, and her reply was, 'Dad, I don't need money to be happy because it makes me happy to make others happy.'

And that was our Carmen.

Carmen then told me about a close friend whose job she'd filled at Eaglehawk Hot Bake. Her friend had to stop working because she had cancer. She was the same age as Jasmine. Every Friday after work, Carmen would go to the girl's house and spend time with her, giving her a gift of some kind. Carmen was devastated, knowing her friend would soon die, but she was happy they had become great friends. Incredibly, Carmen was the first to die.

I'm still alive, and Carmen is dead.
Carmen is dead.

I wondered if the girls could sleep. Mum and Dad, and our house full of extended family. I wondered if anyone could sleep. Carmen hadn't even been dead for 24 hours, and I felt hopeless. Everything was hopeless.

How will we all get through this night?
How will we get through life without Carmen?

I was still going over moments in my head from the day before. Carmen was talking about her braces—she was so excited and was counting down the days until she got her braces off her teeth. Just 12 days to go, and she couldn't wait. She had put up with those damn braces for 12 days short of two years, getting them tightened, altered, and cleaned, and she was so looking forward to getting them off. I could see from time to time that she wouldn't smile because she was conscious of the braces.

Just 12 days to go.

Chapter 5

Our first days without Carmen

It was Sunday morning, 24 hours had gone by, and no one had managed to get much sleep. I looked at Ange, and she just burst into tears. We cuddled. Michelle, Katrina, and Jasmine were already crying, as were most of the cousins. My mum was strong, and her support was amazing. Mum and Dad were both trying to smile and make everyone feel as supported as they could, as parents do. I cannot believe how many tears you can cry without running out.

Most of us didn't eat breakfast, but those who did ate in dribs and drabs. It occurred to me at that moment how different this breakfast was from the many we'd previously shared in our home. I looked at my three girls and their cousins in the kitchen, moving slowly, heavily, around each other. Young people whose happy lives had been shattered, no longer the innocent children we'd brought into the world.

I still saw them as children; up until then, they'd all led happy and carefree lives. These children were now living a nightmare, each remembering Carmen and reaching out for her in shared grief. I couldn't believe how cruel life could be and how, in an instant, normal happy life could be shattered, with no hope of redemption. This was a sad breakfast scene, and I felt hopeless again.

A desperate and hollow feeling grew in my gut and in my heart.

> *How is everyone else seeing this morning?*
> *Is anyone else looking at their children or their partner,*
> *and thinking what I am thinking?*

I was trying to work out what the hell was going on. And then I could feel my anger building.

> *What is God thinking?*
> *What the hell is going on here?*
> *Why would God do this to us?*
> *Why is Carmen dead?*

That morning we attended our regular Sunday mass at our local parish church in Axedale. The whole congregation was shocked, and many people didn't know what to say to us. Some simply gave us a hug or a nod, but I knew what they were saying to us with their actions. They were saying, 'Poor, poor Carmen. And poor, poor you.'

After mass, we went home and gathered up some of the flowers lining the hallway. We'd all written our cards to Carmen because we'd decided that we would visit the tree where Carmen's accident had happened the day before.

We drove to the tree as a family, apprehensive and anxious. When we arrived, we found two of Michelle's close friends attaching a huge, yellow cross to the tree. Although it was confronting to see the cross, it was also a fitting tribute to Carmen as it was bright, colourful, and larger than life. A mountain of flowers had already piled up around the base of the tree.

We stood together, supporting each other, cuddling, crying, and trying to come to terms with all of this. Our lives were in ruins because of this tree — the tree that broke our hearts. Carmen's tree.

I looked at the scene where Carmen had been killed when she hit that damn tree just 24 hours earlier. I could see bits of car, glass, stones, and bark. I stared at the tyre marks, deep grooves in the ground, and the gouges in the tree where the deadly impact had occurred. In the air, I could feel the chaos that must have been there at that exact moment.

There was an eerie sound of noise mixed with deafening quietness. I was imagining Carmen's car and Carmen's body, and I just cried.

I had a gaping hole inside my chest, and it hurt like hell. We were all crying. Ange was crying and shaking again, and it was all too much. Michelle came over and cuddled me, and from that, we formed one big group cuddle, all five of us. A truly devastating family moment.

Before leaving the tree, we looked around. We realised that although the highway was lined with trees, this was the only significantly large tree along this stretch. I kept thinking that if Carmen had left the road anywhere else, she'd still be with us. A hopeless thought. All thoughts are hopeless when facing this sort of tragedy. Because no matter how you think about it, nothing can ever bring her back.

When I returned home, I was shaken. But at least many questions about the accident running through my mind had been answered.

Just like the day before, a steady stream of cars arrived throughout the day. And with each new carload came a fresh flood of tears from our caring visitors. It was a day of deep sadness and mourning for everyone. No one could make any sense of it, and the situation still felt so hopeless and devastating. We were all completely drained of energy. We were all shattered and supporting each other because we were all under this dark cloud together.

Bedtime came again, and although our doctor had given us some sleeping tablets, I didn't take any. So, of course, the night played out much the same as the night before—the bed shaking from Ange's sobbing and my mind racing, thinking all kinds of crazy stuff. My mind was crowded with thoughts, and there was not much room left for sleep.

I telephoned the funeral director on Monday morning and asked when we could come in to be with Carmen. He said it wouldn't be possible that day and asked me to call back the following day. We all wanted to be with Carmen, though we were also very apprehensive. We needed to be with her, hold her hand, say a prayer and tell her how much we loved her.

We need to be with Carmen.
We just need to be with her!

That day we discussed things as a family we had never even considered. We had to arrange a funeral, purchase a cemetery plot, pick out a coffin, and coordinate everything with the funeral home. None of us was in the right frame of mind for any of it.

My God.
We are going to bury our baby girl.

No family should ever have to choose a coffin for their child—it was so confronting. That hour we all spent together was heartbreaking. But car crashes do this to families in Australia every single day.

Inevitably, night-time came again. It was still the worst time of the day. We still had many of our extended family staying with us. People were everywhere, finding any spot to sleep so they could be there to support us as a family because we were all in this together.

The bed started shaking again. Ange was crying, and I still couldn't help. I was trying to get to sleep, and the dark loop of thoughts began again. I was thinking about how Carmen had died, what injuries she sustained, whether she suffered, if she had been in terrible pain, and did she know she was dying. I wondered what my Carmen would look like in the morning when we saw her and said goodbye. I thought about how I would be telling her how much I loved her, that I knew she hadn't meant to do this, and that I forgave her. My heart was racing, thinking of seeing Carmen the following day. I was feeling sick.

Tuesday morning came, and I telephoned the funeral director again and asked what time would be convenient for us to come in. He said, 'John, we've done the best we can with Carmen. But honestly, mate, you can't come in and see her like this, and you can't bring your wife and children in to see Carmen like this. Please remember her the way she was. I'm so sorry, but we can't do any better than what we've done. Please don't come in. I'm sorry.'

I could hear the quiver in his voice and tell how upset he was. I told him we would discuss it as a family and get back to him.

He said, 'If you decide you want to come and see Carmen, you should know that I will need to bandage more than half of her head to cover the injuries'.

I told Ange first, and we both agreed we should take his advice and not view Carmen. We then spoke to the girls, and together we all made the heartbreaking decision not to go and see Carmen. We all agreed if the damage was so bad that they needed to cover Carmen's head, we didn't want to remember her that way. This was a huge decision because we all knew what this meant—we would never see Carmen again. NEVER!

We only wanted to hold Carmen's hand, say goodbye, and pray with her. We wanted to see Carmen one more time, one last time, yet this moment was also taken from us. It just felt cruel. It seemed like we were being punished and could do nothing about it.

The following day at the funeral home was the closest we would get to Carmen ever again. This was it, the only moment we had left with her. We placed our hands on the coffin lid, which had already been fixed shut. We all said a prayer together. We all cried, and we told her how much we loved her. It was so confronting knowing that Carmen was in that coffin.

Privately, I told Carmen I forgave her for what had happened. It was devastating to know we were separated from our beautiful girl by only centimetres of wood. I couldn't stop thinking about what Carmen must have looked like, all alone, inside that coffin.

The funeral director presented Ange with Carmen's jewellery.

Each of the girls received one of Carmen's rings, and they exchanged these for one of their own, which was placed with their letters to be buried with Carmen. We had each written a letter to Carmen to leave with her. We also brought her favourite shirt and a packet of Mentos, which were her favourite lollies. Ange had also purchased five keepsake necklaces with the inscription 'Sisters Forever'. The necklaces were designed to break in half, with one half to be kept by each of us and the other to be buried with Carmen.

We also presented the funeral director with the dress that Ange and the girls picked for Carmen to be buried in. Ange had brought this beautiful dress, and both Jasmine and Carmen had worn it on occasion. It was their shared dress, and this was the perfect dress because Carmen would look beautiful in it.

In the coffin. In *her* coffin.

Carmen is in a coffin.

The next few days passed in a haze. Our extended family went home except for my mum and dad, who were incredible. I would like to think that one day I might be as brave as them if, God forbid, something so tragic were to occur in the future. But I hope never to experience anything like that again in my lifetime.

We had plenty of things to keep us occupied because we had a funeral to arrange—Carmen's. What we were doing was still inconceivable, but we had to do it. We had to put the booklets together. The prayers and songs had to be selected and agreed upon by everyone. That was easy because Carmen had her favourite songs, and we were going to play them for her at her funeral. After all, it was her funeral.

We decided to make a photo board that we would display inside the church on the day of Carmen's funeral. We had so many people coming and going since Carmen's car crash, and many of them were turning up with photos they had of Carmen and leaving them with us. The photo board was on display just inside the front door. Every time another person visited, they marvelled at the collection of photos of Carmen through the various stages of her life.

This board was to return to this position after the funeral and remain there for many months.

We had to prepare the church and were determined to make this a huge celebration of Carmen's life. The girls did a great job preparing things. They placed brightly coloured balloons and streamers strategically and tastefully throughout the church because this funeral was going to be a celebration to remember— a celebration of our bright, beautiful Carmen.

The night before Carmen's funeral, a vigil rosary service was held at St. Therese's Catholic Church on the school grounds where all four of our children attended primary school. Traditionally, a rosary service is a much smaller gathering than a funeral. On this occasion, however, the church was full. All of ours and Carmen's friends, plus our extended family, had returned. It was huge.

The mood was sombre as Michelle, Katrina, Jasmine, and their cousins, Julie, Alison, and Lisa, wheeled Carmen's coffin in from the side door to the front of the altar.

The sombre mood continued as Father Frank Marriott called me forward to sprinkle some holy water onto the coffin. I took the bowl of holy water and sprinkled some over the coffin with the brush provided. Then something suddenly came over me, and I just had to do this one thing. I threw the rest of the holy water over the coffin while saying to Carmen, 'Got ya last!'

Father Marriott, horrified, snatched the bowl out of my hand. He didn't seem to be at all pleased with what I'd just done. Was this appropriate? Who knows! But I did it. There was silence, and then, almost as one, my three girls and their three cousins wheeling the coffin burst into laughter. The entire congregation quickly followed.

I knew Carmen would have appreciated it. No, she would have loved it!

'Got ya last' was a game Carmen and I had often played. And at that moment, it felt natural for me to do what I did, appropriate or not. In those moments when nothing seemed real and everything felt uncomfortable, we all did what we could to cope. For heaven's sake, I was facing my youngest daughter in a coffin. What was appropriate about that?

During the rosary service, our girls took turns placing a sentimental item on Carmen's coffin. They explained why they had chosen each item—her tennis racket, work hat, hairbrush, a cushion from her bed, a packet of Mentos—and why each item was special to Carmen and them. They struggled through this and the Prayers of the Faithful. As one broke down, another would step in to take her place, to carry on. I cried through all of it.

The rosary service ended with Ange's choice of the final song, the very fitting, *A little ray of sunshine* by Brian Cadd and Glenn Shorrock.

Chapter 6

The day we said goodbye

It was 22 November 1995, and the day broke after another restless night in a house full of heartbroken family members. I woke up with the realisation that we would bury our daughter that day.

It was a typically beautiful and warm November day. I got dressed in my dark blue suit while Ange looked beautiful, dressed in a blue sleeveless dress. Michelle wore pale pink pants with a lovely black top, Katrina wore a navy skirt and navy top, while Jasmine wore black pants and had purchased a beautiful cream shirt for the occasion. We looked fantastic, and we were burying Carmen. It was all so very wrong.

But for Carmen's sake, we were all determined to make her funeral a happy occasion, a celebration of her life. And you know what, Carmen would have loved her funeral.

I've since learned that the girls could never bring themselves to wear again the clothes they wore to Carmen's funeral. In their own time, each would donate them to the Salvos.

We travelled as a family in the car from our home at Longlea to St. Therese's Catholic Church in Kennington for the 12:00 pm funeral. Hardly a word was spoken in the car.

When we arrived at the church, the hearse was backed up to the steps of the church. This was so confronting because we knew it was there for Carmen. As we walked towards the church, several people nodded, shook my hand, or put their hand in mine or my shoulder in support. Nothing was said because there was nothing to say.

A huge crowd stood outside the church, and I thought they were just hanging back to let us go in first. When we entered the church, it took my breath away because the church was packed to overflowing. This was massive!

We took our seats in the front pew, with our girls seated between Ange and me. Mum and Dad and our extended family were occupying the pews behind us. I reached back and touched Mum on the hand. I needed to feel the assurance and strength that only a mother can give because this was so devastatingly sad, and I knew what this was doing to my mum.

I could hardly bear to look at Carmen's coffin, which was front and centre before the altar of the church. I just knew that Carmen's lifeless body was in there, and there was no hope, no hope, no hope.

Father Frank Marriott came to the altar, and so began our final heart-wrenching celebration and farewell Mass for Carmen. This was the beginning of the end. I found myself staring at the coffin.

The service was beautiful but a bit of a blur because I just kept looking at the coffin, trying to come to terms with what we were all doing.

I was unable to read Carmen's eulogy—I knew there was no way I could get through it. My youngest brother Gavin bravely took this burden off my shoulders. He gave Carmen a wonderful eulogy that had everyone crying and laughing, remembering her life.

When the service was over, the six brave girls, our three daughters—Michelle, Katrina, and Jasmine—and their three cousins—Julie, Alison, and Lisa—carried Carmen out of the church on their shoulders. The funeral home had been concerned about the girls carrying the coffin and asked that it be wheeled out. However, the girls were having none of that. They were determined to carry Carmen out on their shoulders and did so to one of Carmen's favourite songs, *Stairway to Heaven*, by Led Zeppelin.

They slid the coffin into the back of the hearse, and I watched as the funeral director tried to remove their hands from Carmen's coffin. They didn't want to let her go, and I heard him whisper to them, 'C'mon, girls, you need to let go.'

The look of absolute desperation on the girls' faces as they tried in vain to hold onto their little sister and cousin is something I'll never forget.

It was only then that I took the time to look around. I couldn't believe my eyes. I was at the biggest funeral I had ever seen. There were people everywhere. They were hugging me, kissing me and offering their condolences. They were here for Carmen and us and had come from all over Australia.

Up until that moment, I thought that Carmen was just our little girl. I now realise I underestimated Carmen because she touched many lives and belonged to many people. Everyone at Carmen's funeral had lost someone precious, and it would be a long road to recovery for all of us. Some may never recover.

Ange and I got separated in the crush of people, but family and friends surrounded Ange, and everyone wanted to support us.

I met and exchanged words with so many people that it was a blur. I saw people I hadn't seen or even spoken to for years. Many had come from interstate. It was a wonderful show of support.

We all moved to our cars with encouragement and a hint of urgency from the funeral director. Then it hit me. We were at the front of the dreaded procession to the cemetery. The police seemed to be everywhere. They blocked off roads and were directing traffic away from Carmen's funeral procession. This was an incredible tribute to our little girl.

Few words were spoken on the way to the cemetery because none seemed appropriate. And really, what could we possibly have said to each other?

I had been to so many funerals, but this one was so different for me. It was like a dream. It was almost an out-of-body experience.

When we arrived at the cemetery, Ange and I stood at the end of the hearse, holding hands as we watched our three girls and their three cousins slide the coffin from it. They carefully but purposefully lifted Carmen onto their shoulders again. They were carrying Carmen for the final time.

People were everywhere at the cemetery, and everyone walked slowly toward what would become Carmen's final resting place. Ange and I were just two steps behind our brave girls and their cousins as they carried Carmen through the sea of sad faces, many crying and many with their heads bowed. All too soon, we arrived at our destination—Carmen's plot.

The coffin was placed onto the tape that held it hovering in mid-air above the grave in readiness for its final descent. Father Marriott welcomed everyone and said the final prayers of Carmen's funeral. He blessed Carmen's coffin again.

Then the funeral director stepped forward and flicked the switch that saw Carmen's coffin descend slowly into the grave. I watched as the coffin and Carmen slowly—ever so slowly—and too quickly disappeared. When that switch was flicked again, I was transfixed, staring at that hole in the ground. I held Ange and my girls. It was a time to support each other because this was the end.

Yes, this is the end.

We were all invited to step forward to throw a flower or some dirt into *the* grave. We stepped to the edge of the grave, and it was breathtaking—it was tearing our hearts out.

Pink and yellow carnations lay in wait. I selected a flower, took the time to tell Carmen how much I loved her, and then took aim so that the flower would land on the coffin close to her heart.

Even though we celebrated Carmen's life at the cemetery, everyone was crying. There was so much sadness, so much grief, and so much pain. Nothing good could come out of burying Carmen.

My God, this really is the end!

Father Marriott was magnificent and made everyone feel included in the ceremony. By looking down at Carmen's coffin in the ground and throwing a flower on top of it was wrong for me. I kept thinking that it should not have been happening. She looked so far away—six feet had never looked so deep.

Our family and friends quickly gathered around us to sweep us away from the grave and comfort us. A time when no amount of comfort could ever be enough, but every attempt was appreciated.

I looked at our girls and Ange. I looked at Mum and Dad. And I felt so sad and sorry for all of them, for all of us.

Poor Carmen.

We found it hard to leave the cemetery because we knew we were leaving Carmen and could never get her back. It felt like I was walking out on her. I was her dad and supposed to protect her, but I deliberately and consciously left my little girl behind.

I was overcome with the strangest feeling. Because as I walked away from the grave, it was the first time I believed it was over for Carmen and, therefore, for us. Up until that moment, Carmen was still with us. She was in my life every day because she was in the funeral home, the church, and the hearse. But now, she was in the ground, and we had to leave her there. This truly was the end.

I really have no idea what happened at the wake. There was a sea of faces, but none of it mattered. Don't get me wrong. I appreciated everyone coming and supporting us, joining us at Carmen's service and the wake. But to me, this was just food, and everyone was eating, supporting each other, chatting about old times, and enjoying each other's company. It did not feel right to me.

What are we doing?

People were undoubtedly reminiscing about things they had done with Carmen—at school, in the swimming pool, or on the tennis court. And, for them, I hope it helped. But it didn't mean a thing to me. It felt cold and indifferent, not part of all that had just happened. I couldn't come to terms with what was happening. I felt empty.

A few days after Carmen's funeral, we each received a lock of Carmen's hair in a jar. This was a perfect and much-appreciated gesture from the apologetic and caring funeral director.

This has been the longest and most difficult chapter to write.
I don't know how I finished it,
but I'm glad I did because now I can stop crying.
I'm sorry I left you at the cemetery, Carmen.

Chapter 7

Suddenly a family of five
How do we cope?

Our next chapter of life without Carmen was beginning. Everything had changed, and so dramatically.

My family and I had to pick up the pieces to try and continue our lives without our beautiful Carmen. We tried, but so much had changed. When we walked down the street, and when people spoke to us, it was as if there was a black cloud over our heads. It was like no one wanted to come too close for fear of being pulled under the cloud with us.

People rarely said, 'Hi, how are you? Isn't it a beautiful day?' Instead, it was 'Hi, how are you guys going, how are you coping?' or 'I'm thinking of you, we're praying for you.' We appreciated the kind thoughts because these were difficult times for everyone. We were still grieving, and people knew we were.

People I knew would cross the road when they saw me, so they didn't have to speak to me. Others would just say hello and move on as quickly as possible. I didn't blame them because it must have been hard to know what to say. The same thing happened to Ange and the girls. Friends were moving on.

I experienced something similar after my car crash. People gradually dropped off, and many were no longer in my life. Because their life still goes on. After Carmen's death, more people left our lives. It wasn't their fault. It's not anyone's fault because everyone must get on with their own life.

Of course, we had many more people who stuck by us and provided us with much support and encouragement. These people allowed us to continue our lives and included us in their lives, bringing normality. Their generosity and acceptance allowed all of us to continue with life. Unbeknown to them and us, it was a healing and growth process that was completely natural.

We also received support from the Strathdale-Maristians Cricket Club, who, together with the Sedgwick Cricket Club, presented us with an open-ended voucher for a weekend away. We also received a weekend getaway voucher from the fantastic Connellan family. It is amazing how people process what they believe may be of value in the healing process they knew we would need to get through this. Both vouchers were instrumental in giving us weekend breaks where we could get away and reflect, recharge, and take a breath.

This shift in our lives was a hard one for us. After being such an outgoing family, we quickly became homebodies because it was often uncomfortable for us to go out in public. It felt like people were watching us from afar, not daring to come too close. I lost the desire to go out as we didn't have all that much to celebrate at that time, so home was our haven.

Life changed rapidly. Katrina moved back from Sydney. She resigned from the job she had worked hard to get but knew she could not live in Sydney. She needed to be close to her family.

A few weeks after Carmen's funeral, I flew to Sydney with Katrina, where we packed all her belongings. Together we drove back to Longlea in her car. Driving home, we saw the most beautiful rainbow, making us feel like Carmen was travelling with us.

Together we supported each other through these tough days, weeks, and agonisingly long months. I made an appointment for the five of us to see Ivan Honey, the counsellor who had helped me so much following my crash. I knew we would need help to put things in perspective and to come to terms with the loss of Carmen. None of the girls really connected with Ivan. However, I continued to see him regularly and would continue to do so for several years.

We all knew Michelle needed help most of all—she'd seen her little sister in that car, but we couldn't force her to get therapy. We all did our best to support Michelle. However, she had her heart set on escaping the reality of life without Carmen. She had begun planning an overseas trip to Europe, which included visiting a friend living in Greece.

Shortly after Carmen's funeral, we began talking about what we would do with Carmen's life insurance. Ange and I decided that Carmen would want her sisters to have it. We discussed things like buying each of them a car or giving them money towards a house deposit. Another option we floated was that the three girls could travel overseas together. From Ange's and my point of view, it would mean that Trin and Jasmine would be there to continue to support Michelle, who was still struggling. I remember sitting next to Ange on Carmen's bed with the three girls around us. We discussed this could be an opportunity for them to take Carmen with them and show her all the places she would never get to see. It would also be a chance for the girls to do something together that they would remember forever.

The overseas trip was certainly the option that Michelle wanted. With some persuading, Trin and Jasmine agreed they should go and see the world for Carmen. The trip gave the girls, and Ange and me something positive and meaningful to focus on, and the planning began in earnest in mid-December. The first trip to the travel agency in Bendigo resulted in the girls discovering that for only an extra few hundred dollars a ticket, they could buy themselves a round-the-world ticket and see a whole lot more for Carmen. The girls went from planning a trip to Europe to planning a 16-week backpacking—YES, backpacking—trip to America, Europe, and Africa.

My three girls are backpacking.
Around the world.
Alone.
Only months after losing their sister.

For the first time since Carmen's crash, and through planning this adventure, I saw the girls with some spirit. The round-the-world trip was booked for March 1996, just four short months after we lost Carmen. Before they left, the girls organised a 'Doing the Skip' party to say goodbye to all their family and friends. It was huge. Our extended family and many friends made the trek to Bendigo for the party, and we all had a fantastic night. Everyone let loose. My brothers, of course, were a disgrace, which was perfect, and to be expected.

This was exactly what the doctor ordered. All of us were together again, for the first time since Carmen's funeral, and we were able to let our hair down. Although the pain was still there, we at least had something to celebrate as a family. Something we all needed so desperately because you can only survive for so long in complete darkness.

At that point, neither Ange nor myself had considered how this trip might impact us. I recall the night before the girls were due to leave, and the reality of it all hit me. I walked into Carmen's room and saw Jasmine packing the last of her items into her backpack, and I burst into tears. It wasn't long before Michelle, Trin, and Ange were in Carmen's room with us, and I stammered that I didn't think they should go. I was scared that having just lost Carmen, I might lose them too. It was then that the girls firmly stated the trip was booked. Michelle was going to go regardless, and they wanted to do this together for Carmen.

This backpacking adventure was planned to take four months, and it wasn't long after the girls left on their trip that Ange and I realised just how hard things were going to get for us. Those four long months were tough on both of us. We were mourning Carmen and lost without our girls. It was so quiet and lonely in our big home—it was horrible. Our only consolation was that at least our girls were having some fun and an adventure, something they had been unable to do at home.

They were all languishing in the sadness of losing their baby sister and were not enjoying life in general at home. One thing I knew for certain was that Carmen would not have wanted to see that happen to her sisters. So, the trip was important and timely.

Ange and I put money on a phone card before the girls left, and we made them promise to telephone us every three days to let us know how things were going. We needed to know they were safe. This plan was working beautifully. The girls were timing their calls perfectly, and we enjoyed hearing about their travels. Until one morning, when we were woken up, startled by a call at an unsociably early 4:00 am. Ange and I were both fast asleep. We had the phone near the bed in case of an emergency. So, of course, when the phone rang at such an early hour, I grabbed the phone, sat bolt upright in bed, and quickly answered. It was Katrina.

'Hi, Dad! Did I wake you up?'

'Err, yes, you did, but that's ok. Is everything all right?'

'Yes, but two of your daughters are a disgrace!'

'Why, what's going on?'

My concern started to build. What were my daughters up to?

They were so far away. If they were in immediate trouble, I wouldn't be able to help.

'We're in New Orleans, and Michelle and Jaz are dancing on the bar!' It was now obvious to me that Trin had had a few drinks.

I'd been to New Orleans some years earlier and had seen the signs everywhere, warning they would be arrested if anyone was caught dancing on the bar. I demanded that Katrina get her sisters down from the bar, 'They'll get arrested!'

'I can't because every time we try to get down, the police help put us back up there,' she blurted out and then burst into laughter.

Our three girls were becoming very well known as the three Australian sisters backpacking around the world. People were looking out for them, protecting them. They were safe and having a ball. This made me feel so much better.

Before they left for their adventure, I spoke to someone who made the same train trip the girls had booked across America. They told me the story of someone they knew who had all their luggage stolen on that train journey when sleeping gas was pumped into their carriage. Apparently, this was a common occurrence, and many people lost their luggage and passports in this manner.

Of course, as a dad, I purchased lengths of chain and some padlocks and made the girls promise to padlock the carriage door shut when they slept on that train. The girls said they heard someone trying to open the carriage door one night, but they didn't get in, thanks to the locks. I don't know if my cautiousness saved them from losing their luggage, but I'd like to think so!

Our girls had an amazing experience, and we were delighted they had it together. We knew it was special, and they would forever have this 'backpacking bond' between them.

Every time they called, they were telling us things that amazed us, and sometimes things that didn't please us too much. One such story was when they arrived in Amsterdam during a music festival and couldn't get accommodation. So, they rolled out their air mattresses and slept together under the lights outside a public toilet block in the park!

But there was one phone call I will never forget. The girls were on their final leg, with only weeks to go on their trip. We were so thrilled to know they were on their way back to us. They were in Turkey when we received a phone call from Katrina. She told us Michelle wasn't going to come home to Australia. She said Michelle was getting anxious and felt she couldn't come home and face everything, so she wasn't going to come home.

We need to get all of our girls home.

We contacted the Traffic Accident Commission, or TAC, and explained our plight. I explained that Michelle wasn't coping, and it was all to do with Carmen's death. The TAC was helpful and agreed this was a trauma response related to Carmen's car crash. The TAC then paid for Ivan Honey to counsel Michelle over the phone throughout the last weeks of the trip. Ivan proved invaluable to us as a family because he helped Michelle to find the strength to return home to Australia.

Ange and I were so happy when our girls arrived home and were safe. These had been the longest four months of our lives, and finally, they were over. The girls were home, and we could get on with picking up the pieces and rebuild our lives together as a family. The girls had an experience of a lifetime, and so had Ange and I.

We never told the girls how much we struggled over those four months. We spent a lot of time at the cemetery and what was widely known as 'Carmen's tree', and we remembered. It was tough, but we thanked God we had each other because it was so lonely without our girls. Without all four of them!

We were all back together again, without our dear Carmen, ready to tackle the next phase of life. We knew it would be difficult as so much had changed, but we didn't quite realise how difficult things would be.

We saw a huge change in our girls, particularly in Michelle. They were no longer the happy-go-lucky Maher girls of yesterday, going out socialising and partying, which was what girls their age should have been doing. Michelle seemed to have regressed the most and hardly ever went out socially.

One day Carmen's best friend, Carmen Trevean, telephoned and told Michelle she couldn't stay home for the rest of her life. She said she was going to take Michelle out for a drink in Bendigo, and she wouldn't take no for an answer. Michelle agreed, and the two set out for a night on the town. They were having a great time at the nightclub, catching up with many friends, when a school friend came over to Michelle and Carmen and mistook Michelle for our Carmen. He was so used to seeing the two Carmen's together and exclaimed, 'Carmen, someone told me you were killed in a car crash?'

Carmen Trevean replied angrily, 'This is Michelle. And Carmen did die in a car crash, you idiot.'

The poor young fellow burst into tears, and so did Michelle and Carmen. That was the end of the night out and was the last time Michelle went out in Bendigo for months.

Yes, these were tough times—everything was still so raw.

Part 3

Looking back to look forward

Chapter 8

Michelle's memories

Written by Michelle

Pressing my hands on the glass window, looking in, I could see Carmen wrapped tightly in the hospital blanket. All I wanted was a little brother, as I already had two sisters. I thought a brother would have been a nice change. That thought evaporated as I had my own real-life baby girl doll. I remember thinking how much fun it was going to be, dressing her up, giving her baths, and helping Mum. I was only six years old, but I melted at the sight of her.

As the years went by, I found myself quite protective of Carmen. Being the youngest, she was a baby for a long time. At night we all struggled with nightmares, and Carmen would jump into bed with me while Jasmine would jump in with Katrina. This only stopped when I was about 14 years old, making Carmen eight at the time. We were all very close. We had the odd barney at times, but all in all, we were best friends.

We were lucky to have been brought up on a wonderful property. We were not spoilt, but we were grateful to have been given two ponies for Christmas. Although Dad had bred and raced pacers all our lives, this was different. We would have races, do a jumps course, or just hang out with our horses, Jonathan and Spike. I think Mum and Dad were quite smart, as these ponies kept us girls playing outside for most of our childhood.

I completed my secondary schooling and, at 18, started my

hairdressing apprenticeship. I had to grow up fast. Life became exciting and exhausting. I absolutely loved my work but found that I didn't get to see my friends as often as I wanted. Sunday was the main family day at home. By then, we were all growing up and visiting friends, and Carmen always had sleepovers at her friend Carmen Trevean's. They were best friends.

The years began to blend, and time was flying. Suddenly life changed. I was home with my sisters and a good friend. Dad had left to go to a cricket club function, as they celebrated the cricket final they had just won. I answered the phone to be told by a family friend that Dad had been involved in a serious car accident and was still trapped in the car. I remember screaming and dropping the phone.

That afternoon we learned that Dad was freed from the wreck but had serious facial injuries. The following day we were able to see him, but he had facial surgery and a face full of plates and screws.

After the accident, Dad was so swollen and bruised. I was in a state of shock, thankful to have him in our lives but scared to look at him. I didn't want this for my dad or our family.

Life was suddenly different, as Dad had short-term memory problems, a legacy of his car crash, which made him difficult to live with at times.

We all stuck together and helped him through it. After all, it wasn't Dad's fault his life had been turned upside down.

I had my 21st birthday party at home, which was a blast. Things were settling at home, and Dad was adjusting to his new life. Unable to work due to his injuries, the only positive was that he could watch movies over and over, as he couldn't remember them. I had no idea that a brain injury could be so challenging and change a person so much until it happened to Dad. I suppose I never had that worry.

In 1993, I moved out of the home to be closer to work and to have my independence.

I soon realised I was a rotten cook who hated washing my clothes and needed to budget down to the last cent. I got a second job to help with the budget and went on a good holiday. After a year, I decided to move back home to save some money and go overseas to visit my best friend, Paula. I'm sure most children in their 20s do this at some stage.

Moving back home in 1995 was wonderful. I loved the open space and the smell of eucalyptus in the air. I had just broken up with my boyfriend of over four years, and although I was going to miss our beautiful relationship, I felt it was for the best. Our lives were going in different directions, and mine was hopefully heading overseas.

Although Katrina was living in Sydney by then, and Jasmine had entered university in Geelong, Carmen was still living at home. I was only home for two days when Carmen surprised us by coming home with a kitten, Tex. He was a ripper, fluffy and cute. It was nice to sit and reconnect with Carmen after having been out of home for so long. Nothing had changed us, we were still mates, but now both worked full time—Carmen at the Eaglehawk Hot Bake, me still hairdressing.

We chatted about her work and how great it was to have your own money and to be a part of people's lives. Carmen enjoyed chatting to customers as much as I did. I felt I had left home when Carmen was still a little girl and when I moved back, she had grown into a beautiful young lady. And I told her so.

They were precious days. Six in total.

On Friday night, it was the Bendigo Cup. We went as a family and had our mates with us. It truly was a day to remember. Laughter and fun, and a few drinks. That night we all went to the nightclubs and had a ball. We danced all night. I bought Carmen and her best friend Carmen Trevean a soft drink each before I had to go. I dearly wanted to stay on and party for a few more hours, but I had to work the following morning. Home I went, telling them to have a great night.

The next morning, as usual, I was running late for work. I ran through the door into the kitchen and was surprised to see Carmen asleep with her head resting on the table. When I woke her and told her to go back to bed, she said she had to drive Carmen Trevean to work.

I said, 'I can take her on my way to work. You're tired and should go back to bed.'

Just then, Carmen Trevean walked into the kitchen and said, 'Okay, I'm ready to go.'

I looked at Carmen and said, 'I will be ready in five minutes. I can do it.'

She laughed and said she would be fine. It all happened quickly, but something inside me knew it didn't feel right. I told her to put the music on, wind the window down and gave her the thumbs up. I watched the two Carmens' get in the car and waved. They were laughing as teenagers do, and I thought nothing else of it.

Walking, then running, down the hall, I rushed to get ready for work. Saturday mornings were always busy. I started my car, and the strangest feeling came over me—I had to wear a little daisy clip in my hair that I had bought the week before. It was dainty with tiny little petals but nothing expensive or special. I told myself 'no' as I didn't have time. Then the feeling grew, and I said 'okay'.

Running down the hallway again, shaking my head because I couldn't believe I was doing that, I grabbed the hair clip, ran back to the car, and said aloud, 'Is that better now?'

Crazy, I know, but I have always talked to my mum's father, an elderly dairy farmer. He loved his hothouse full of spectacular flowers. He was my pop who died when I was only seven. I have always found comfort in chatting with him and still do to this day.

I remember looking at the beautiful day—clear blue skies and warm sun on my cheek as I drove. Five minutes into my drive to work, I had a bad feeling—I should have passed Carmen by then. That feeling grew to terror, and I started to cry. I blinked, and although I can't explain how it happened, I pictured Carmen's car crash. I screamed, started to shake, and howled, 'NO!' I drove over the hill, and there was my shocking vision. I knew Carmen was in the car, crumpled up on the side of the road next to the only large tree. I can't remember parking my car, but I remember asking Pop over and over again—why?

I got out of my car and looked at the two police officers talking to a lady, and a small boy, standing on the opposite side of the road.

Then a man and his young boy came over to me. He told me I shouldn't be there, that there had been an accident.

'This is no place for you, and you must leave,' he said.

I can vividly remember thinking, why would he have his child around this? How strange. Then it occurred to me that Carmen must be ok. They must be waiting for the ambulance.

I said through tears, 'I know, it's my sister. Is she ok?'

With that, the man ran off across the road with his son and got the older police officer.

I was striding towards the car. Praying to see that Carmen wasn't inside but already on her way to the hospital. The police officer was suddenly by my side. He stopped me, and I said, 'That's my sister in that car. Is she ok?'

He just looked at me for what felt like years. So, I simply walked past him. He grabbed me gently by the arm, and this time, I screamed, 'Is Carmen okay? I'm going to take her home.'

I truly don't remember if he said anything, but if so, I didn't hear it. I punched him in the face and broke free of his grasp to get Carmen out of the car. This time he grabbed me by the upper arms with more force. He looked me in the eyes and said, 'I'm sorry, but your sister is deceased.'

I just looked at him and said, 'No, that's not right, that's my sister, and I'm taking her home.'

I turned and looked at the car. This time I could see Carmen lying under a single white sheet, but she was on the passenger side. I could see, but I didn't want to believe it.

I began to hear a sound coming from deep within me, a sound I had never heard before and a sound I never wanted to hear again. It was the sound of me breaking for Carmen and realising her death was my fault. Our Carmen was gone. I can only describe the sound as a low grumble that grew into a screaming howl. All I could say over and over was 'NO, NO, NO'. I was trembling, I remember thinking. Not our little Carmen. I felt weak at the knees and distant.

I felt the police officer supporting me, his arms gently around me as I sobbed into his shoulder. I'm not sure how much time passed.

I just couldn't control myself. I was rocking, shaking, and sobbing. I looked over at Carmen and just hoped that she hadn't suffered. I stepped back, and the police officer asked me if I could identify Carmen from her licence. I said yes, through tears pouring down my face. How could this be happening? And, my God, this was all my fault. I had let her drive. I hung my head in shame, waiting for the police officer to return.

He walked over holding Carmen's little elephant handbag; I knew this was real. Again, tears flowed freely down my face, and I didn't care. He opened it up, gave me the licence, and asked, 'Is that your sister?'

I simply said, 'Yes.'

I asked the police officer if I could hold Carmen's hand to say goodbye. I think I was begging him. He said no. He told me he had a few things to do and would be back as soon as possible. I stood only three short steps away from my youngest sister's lifeless body. I turned to look where the police officer was. He was still on the opposite side of the road, talking to the lady and her son.

The urge grew for me to ignore what the police officer had just said and to open the door and be with Carmen. To hold her hand for the last time. It was just three small steps.

I took a step forward, and my body began to shake uncontrollably. I was terrified of what Carmen might look like under that white sheet. I stood there, suddenly frozen in fear and unable to hold her hand. I thought of Carmen with her perfect skin, beautiful blue eyes, thick wavy hair, and stinking bloody braces, which she hated.

Carmen was excited and looking forward to them being removed for good in only two weeks. She never made it. I wept, trembling, placing my head in my hands.

What have I done?
I'm so sorry, Carmen.
I'm your big sister, and I have let you down.
I have let everybody down.
This is all my fault.
This is all my fault.

I questioned God and Pop. Why Carmen? Why not me? I had lived my life and wanted it to be me, not Carmen. Why Carmen? Why hadn't she been given a warning, a second chance like all the drunk drivers who had horrendous accidents and walked away unharmed? Carmen was so innocent and young, with her life ahead of her. Why?

I was swaying. A young police officer was beside me out of nowhere. He said, 'Maybe sitting in the police car would be better.'

I felt rooted to the spot and didn't want to leave Carmen alone. She was only 18, our baby. It wasn't supposed to be like this. I couldn't move. I stood, staring blankly at the young police officer.

He came and stood next to me and gestured toward the police car. I glanced over and remembered Mum and Dad were on their way into Bendigo to do a tin-shake for the Spastic Society of Victoria. I told the police officer that we had to get home immediately, to stop them from coming here and seeing Carmen like that.

The police officer placed me in the police car on the opposite side of the road to Carmen. I looked across and could still see into her car. As he walked away, I screamed. 'What have we done to deserve this?'

First Dad, then Carmen.

I punched the back of the seat, and then I kicked it. I screamed and screamed. The young police officer returned and said, 'This is not a good place for you. I will move the car up and be back with you soon.'

I could feel people looking at me. I saw the lady and her young son talking to the older police officer. When the young police officer returned, I asked him, 'Who are they?'

He replied, 'They are the people your sister's car veered across the road in front of. The lady saw your sister's head down on her chest and thought she was asleep.'

It was true. It was because of me that Carmen was dead. She had become warm and comfortable with the beautiful sun shining on her face. I felt it earlier in the morning. Now I felt nothing but regret.

Why didn't this woman blast the horn at Carmen? I felt myself becoming worked up and so, so angry. It may have saved her life. Then reality hit. The horn may have woken Carmen up, and she would have been terrified and scared, knowing she was going to hit the tree. Or just as horrifying, Carmen may have swerved back onto the road, possibly killing the lady and her young boy or all three of them.

I felt sick. I just wanted this to go away.

The police officer returned, and we drove home. I remember having waves of tears that never stopped. I told the young police officer this would kill Dad, as he had just been through a car accident that wasn't his fault, and he wasn't right; he wasn't well. His brain was just not right. He was going to kill himself. It was all my fault. I let Carmen drive, and I knew she was tired. Then I buried my face in my hands and screamed, 'What have I done?' For some reason, I looked in the rear-view mirror and realised this upset the police officer. I looked away, thinking, who would be a cop. What a shit job that must be, seeing families destroyed in the blink of an eye.

We turned into the driveway, and Mum and Dad were standing at the back of their car. Seeing them placing the posters in the boot seemed so ridiculous to me. We were fundraising because I had decided, at the beginning of the year, to help others. Dad had had a horrible accident, but nothing truly bad happened to us. I wanted to give back to others, to make their lives better. I had Mum, Dad, Katrina, Jasmine, and Carmen's full support. It had been a great year, and we all enjoyed it. But my heart was aching as I watched the confusion wash over their faces when they saw the police car. They walked over, and I was petrified. I froze in the back seat.

The police officer got out of the car, and I could hear Dad questioning him. Then Mum joined Dad. I could see their faces, and I knew they were like me earlier, not understanding. I could hear the police officer saying Carmen had been involved in a car accident.

Then Dad called out to me, saying, 'Carmen! Get out of the car. It's ok!'

I thought, 'Oh God, Dad thinks I'm Carmen.' I knew I was going to have to say the hardest words of my life.

I took a long deep breath and then slowly steadied myself. I got out of the car and saw confusion wash over Mum and Dad's faces. Then Dad asked, 'Michelle, what's going on?'

I held out both my hands, with my palms to the sky, and said, 'It's Carmen, Dad. Carmen's gone. Carmen's dead.'

My tears didn't seem to stop, and I couldn't control myself.

I watched my parent's hearts break and their lives shattered before my eyes. I said, 'I'm sorry.'

Mum screamed, and they grabbed for each other. They clung to each other for support. My God. It was a nightmare, a real-life nightmare.

Dad was saying, 'Where has this happened? I need to go to Carmen.'

I screamed, 'Dad, don't go there, please don't go there, Dad.'

I could hear the police officer saying, 'I think we need to go inside.'

I turned to see Jasmine collapse to the ground screaming, falling on her side and then on her back. I ran to her as fast as I could, to be by her side. I dropped to the ground and gently picked little Jasmine up in my arms, cradling her. I looked to the sky and asked, 'Why Carmen, why?' Jasmine and I were together on the ground, and we sobbed for Carmen.

I turned to see the young police officer guiding Mum and Dad towards the house. The same gesture he had shown me earlier at Carmen's accident scene. We followed him inside the house in total disbelief, with broken hearts. My God, what had just happened? It seemed so unreal.

This shouldn't have been happening to us.

Inside, Dad paced the kitchen and kicked the footstool straight across the room into the glass door. The door didn't break, but I was so scared. I had never witnessed anything like that from my dad, ever. That sound was deafening.

I walked down to the bathroom and vomited in the toilet. I was shaking my head and looking in the mirror as I washed my hands. That little clip in my hair had stopped me, possibly preventing Carmen from hitting that bloody tree. This was my fault. I felt like

I wanted to die, never wake up, and not face life. What had I done?

I turned the taps off and walked straight into Carmen's bedroom. I had one thing on my mind—to find the 18th birthday card that I had given Carmen. On it, I had written for her to enjoy her freedom with her car. To enjoy being of legal age, going out and having fun with her friends, and just enjoying life. But I had also written, 'Don't pick on a bigger tree.' I had written that as a joke. When Carmen was learning to drive, she bumped into a little tree in the front yard. I had gone out to make sure she was ok, and she was. We then went over her little Honda Civic, but not a scratch was to be found. We both roared with laughter and couldn't believe she had hit the tree going only five kilometres per hour.

I found the card beside her bed, on a shelf with all her other cards. I took it in my hand and re-read it, 'Don't pick on a bigger tree.' I screamed and ripped it into tiny pieces. I hated myself, I hated my life, and I was so sorry for Carmen. Had I known this was going to happen? The feeling I had that morning—that Carmen shouldn't drive—flooded my mind. I had to tell Mum and Dad. This wasn't Carmen's fault—it was all mine. I shouldn't have let her drive in the first place.

I went into the kitchen to explain to Mum and Dad how I had found Carmen asleep at the table that morning but that she had wanted to drive Carmen Trevean to work. They had taken Mum's car, and I was so sorry Carmen was too tired to drive. I told Mum and Dad I should have woken them up and that I was sorry. Again, we were all crying.

The police officer asked if we wanted tea or coffee. I remember thinking I didn't give a crap about tea or coffee. I just wanted my sister back. Soon after that, he left, saying he would be back. He is someone I will remember for the rest of my life, for all the wrong reasons. What a brave young police officer, choosing to be part of such chaos and heartbreak.

Dad rang Katrina as she was working in Sydney, and it was horrible to watch. I had to walk away. Then Dad called his parents and the rest of our family. Within the day, we had all our loved ones by our side to face this together. All we did was cry and support each other. I will forever love my extended family and closest friends. I don't think they realised how much we needed their love and support to help us through that intense first day, full of grief and sorrow.

The Monday following Carmen's accident, when Dad asked the funeral director if we could view Carmen, I had another meltdown. I knew Carmen wouldn't look like our Carmen and my mind was anxious about what we might see. The funeral director said we could visit, but he would have to bandage up half of her head. Again, we cried. How could that be? At his recommendation, we decided it was best to remember her the way she was. I was so relieved, as my dreams were already grotesque, and I had begun to dread the thought of sleep.

We didn't view Carmen—we chose a coffin instead. We stood there looking at all the different timbers for coffins, the satin linings, and all the different crosses to go on top. I just felt angry, so angry that I wanted to kick them all over and smash the crap out of them. I knew that wasn't the right thing to do, so I left and sat outside.

We then had to organise the church booklet, and I found it surprisingly rewarding to be able to place Carmen's favourite songs into the booklet. I felt Carmen would have been happy with our efforts.

The day of the funeral was dreadful. It was just so hard to believe that we were about to bury my youngest sister, someone who should have outlived me, as I was the oldest.

I stood in my room, wardrobe open, not knowing what to wear. What was appropriate to wear to bury my sister? I stood again with my head in my hands and cried for Carmen. Mum walked in and helped me choose an outfit. I was 23 years old but couldn't get myself dressed that day. To be honest, I didn't take much notice. I put on the black top and pale pink pants and thought, is this appropriate for burying my youngest sister? Who knew? I still don't know.

When we drove up to the church, there were people everywhere, even outside the church. Carmen was popular, and we all knew it. I remember thinking I couldn't go in, but we were all there for each other, giving each other strength, and we got through it.

The one thing we had all decided on was that we would carry Carmen out of the church. It was physically and emotionally difficult but so fulfilling and rewarding, knowing that I was performing one final act of love for Carmen. And I was proud to have the help of my sisters and cousins. The weight of the coffin and Carmen was extremely heavy, something I hadn't given much thought to. I wondered if the girls were handling the weight and thinking the same. Was it because I hadn't slept and felt weak? All I could think was, this is for you, Carmen, and I'm very sorry. I could see Carmen's dear friends in front of me as we walked out of the church, with Carmen high up on our shoulders. I felt sorry for everyone who loved Carmen as much as we did.

At the burial, the wave of nausea came over me again, and I felt like I was going to faint. It was all so final. That was it, I thought; it was all done with. Carmen was gone.

I looked down and said to Carmen as she was lowered into the ground, 'You will never be forgotten. I hate this place and may never be back, but I will always chat with you and Pop. I hope you are happy together, and I will see you soon, one day'.

I struggled to know what to do with myself after Carmen's death. I had one week off work and needed to go back. I couldn't be alone and idle. I was consumed with thoughts of Carmen and what transformations her body was going through—the aftermath of death and what happens to a corpse, weird stuff. To be honest, I think I was going crazy, and I couldn't tell anyone.

I became a homebody. I wasn't going out as I had had a few bad experiences with people crying in front of me, obviously feeling sorry for me. One poor teenage boy thought I was Carmen. The worst moments were when friends simply didn't know what to say, so they walked away. It wasn't their fault. It was just too confronting for them. I tried to stay in touch with my dear friends, but unfortunately for some, we drifted apart. It was no one's fault. I think about it from time to time, but life changes and people change, and that's ok.

Life felt pointless in so many ways. I didn't care about anything. I felt I deserved to be alone after what I had done to poor Carmen. I enjoyed playing with Carmen's little kitten, Tex. He was gorgeous and the only thing that made me smile.

It was the final of the Australian Open tennis in 1996, and for some reason, I didn't want to watch it at home. I dragged Mum to

Ballarat, where we watched it at my uncle Gavin's house with his wife Julie, who was overdue with their second baby. After a few drinks, Gav and I went to meet up with Katrina, Jasmine, and my cousins. Somehow, and only three short months after Carmen's death, I met a lovely potato and dairy farmer from Bungaree. Yes, that's right, from Dad's hometown.

Life was crazy. There was no way I felt I deserved to be having a wonderful time and being shown any form of affection. And so, I began to lead a double life. Tony knew about Carmen's death, and I told him only what he needed to know. I couldn't tell him how devastated and heartbroken I was, as he had never met Carmen. He didn't know the person I was mourning.

Only six weeks later, Katrina, Jasmine, and I went on a trip around the world. I enjoyed it, but my mind was haunting me. I couldn't sleep and felt it was exactly what I deserved, so I still didn't tell anyone. In Turkey, I had a breakdown and refused to return home. I was scared to face it all again. Every day I would have to face driving past the massive old gum tree that took Carmen's life. I couldn't face it. Thankfully, Katrina and Jasmine had spoken to Mum and Dad, and they organized for a psychologist to call. After a chat with him, I understood it was ok to have trepidation and that it was natural after going through the trauma of Carmen's death. We agreed that when I got home, he would help me through my feelings and try to get me sleeping again. That chat worked. I made it home and slipped straight back into my double life.

The next chat I had with the psychologist didn't go as smoothly. Unfortunately, I was a bit of a lost cause. I asked him if he had ever seen his younger sister or brother dead in a car. When he replied 'No' I told him. 'That's why you can't help me. You don't understand.'

Looking back now, I know he was exactly the person I needed to talk to. But at the time, I didn't want to talk about it to anyone, let alone a stranger. Poor Ivan!

The time I spent with my spud farmer, Tony, was a breath of fresh air, but when I was by myself, I was a bawling mess. I didn't want to worry Mum and Dad, as they were still in massive pain themselves. My decision to let Carmen drive that morning was still haunting my every waking moment, and I felt it snowballing. I had begun to shake and have heart palpitations, so much so that at times I thought I had a heart attack. These panic and anxiety attacks left me feeling weak and unable to function properly. But again, I felt I deserved this for what I had done to Carmen.

I was unaware that this was depression, and I was doing a great job hiding it from the world. Well, I thought I was. There were times when I'd go for a drive by myself, thinking of ending it all, that life wasn't worth living, and I couldn't see any meaning in it. But I knew if I did, the only people I would be hurting were Mum and Dad. I knew they wouldn't be able to go through the loss of another child, and they were my only concern. I wondered if there was ever going to be a day when I stopped caring and it would all be over. I found myself thinking about suicide and how lost and alone a person must feel to follow through with the final act.

After two years, I decided I did have a future. That future was with Tony, and I had to get myself out of the mess. I began meditation classes, but I found the first few sessions frustrating. I wasn't good at relaxing. After learning the importance of deep breathing, I started to enjoy it and, for the first time, enjoyed a safe and sound full night of sleep. It wasn't every night, but a few full nights of sleep per week were better than a few hours per night. I also realised I had a big problem and needed professional help, so I took myself off to see a psychologist. Suddenly, I could see that life had meaning. I had my life, and I was going to make the most of it for Carmen. I would never forget her, but I was finally in a place where I could live with my thoughts and my mind.

I had made the decision to travel around Australia that year and was thrilled when Tony said he would join me. The west coast of Australia was a memorable time, and we thoroughly enjoyed the beauty of this magnificent country.

In the year 2000, Tony and I married. Then two years later, when I heard the first cry of my newborn daughter, Jaida, a weight lifted from my soul. So, it took me just over six years from the date of Carmen's death to forgive myself, and that was thanks to Jaida entering my life.

On reflection, I know there is no changing the path of life. I had been to some very dark places, and I know I was sometimes lost.

Eventually, I learned that the best thing to do was to ask for help from a psychologist.

Depression, anxiety, and panic attacks are still part of my life, but I understand how to manage them, whether with medication or relaxation techniques. I was very private about these very personal struggles. I hope that by sharing my journey in Carmen's Legacy, by expressing my feelings and saying it's ok to have mental health issues, and that I now understand how others suffer in this way, I hope they can find the courage to seek help like I have. I sought help from different psychologists until I found the one who understood me and was able to help me.

I know Mum and Dad have never blamed me for Carmen's death. But I am the one who must live with the decisions that I made that morning, and I must live with them for the rest of my life.

Chapter 9

Carmen's tree

It was 18 November 1996, the first anniversary of Carmen's death, a day I had been dreading. We planned to be at the tree where Carmen had died by 8:08 am, in remembrance of the very moment that Carmen lost her life.

It was a sombre mood in our house that morning, as expected. Ange and the girls were teary as we tried to eat breakfast and prepare to make the dreaded journey to what we all now called 'Carmen's tree'. I had mixed emotions. I was feeling down but also looking forward to us being at the tree as a family to remember.

When we arrived at Carmen's tree with our fresh bunches of flowers, we immediately noticed there were more flowers than usual. Carmen's tree had been adorned with flowers since that fateful day, 12 months earlier. It was rare for any family, or Carmen's friends, to visit here without bringing flowers or a present. Various ornamental angels, dogs, cats, pigs, and pixies surrounded the tree. Every so often, we would find a packet of Mentos, Carmen's favourite lollies, at the base of the tree. People were always thinking of her.

We placed our flowers and a few trinkets at the base of the tree and said some prayers for Carmen. Ange, Michelle, Katrina, and Jasmine were all crying. I was fighting back tears, trying to be strong.

As we stood at Carmen's tree, a family united in tragedy, cars on the highway slowed as they passed. And with Bendigo being just like a big country town, I had no doubt that many of the occupants in those cars knew who we were and exactly what we were doing there. I wondered if any of them could comprehend what we were feeling. I wondered if they could see our broken hearts as they drove past.

Although the year had not been easy, putting ourselves back at the exact moment, on the exact day, at the exact place we lost Carmen, was harrowing for all of us. While the girls and I stood together at the tree, arm in arm, remembering the horrific event that had taken place, I found myself looking at the small embankment that had grabbed the bottom of Carmen's car. This embankment had turned Carmen's car just enough so that Carmen's door—the driver's—had crashed squarely into the trunk of the tree, killing Carmen instantly.

I touched the deep gouges left in the trunk of the tree by Carmen's car.

Before we left, we tidied up around the tree. Nothing much was said. Instead, we were all consumed with our own private thoughts. We were all thinking of Carmen and wishing this horrible event had never happened. I kept looking at that damn embankment, thinking if it hadn't been there, Carmen would have missed the tree and gone through the fence into a cleared paddock.

I looked at that bloody tree again, and I touched the gouges. Permanent reminders of the damage Carmen's car did to the tree but insignificant compared to the damage the tree did to Carmen.

Carmen's tree wasn't just a place we visited on her anniversary. The scene of Carmen's accident was on the route of our daily commute into Bendigo. We drove past Carmen's tree morning and night, and it was a constant reminder of our tragic loss. Although this was difficult, I found solace at the tree because it was the last place that Carmen was alive. For me, it held more significance than the cemetery.

In the following years, I made certain we were at Carmen's tree by 8:00 am on that fateful November day. This is so we could be present and remember the 8:08 am car crash that took Carmen from us. I don't know if people think this to be morbid, childish, or just stupid, but this is what I needed to do. Ange wouldn't have come with me unless she felt it was necessary as well, or perhaps she did it to support me. I've never asked. Four years after the accident, we moved to Ballarat to be closer to our children and grandchildren, and the need for this ritual ceased.

Now we only visit when we are in Bendigo, and we rarely go to Bendigo without visiting Carmen's tree.

Chapter 10

Carmen's Racing Syndicate

Written by Jasmine

Two and a half months before we lost Carmen, a feisty little chestnut filly was born at home. Unfortunately, this foal didn't get a lot of attention early on. We were still reeling from the loss of Carmen, so there wasn't a lot of interest in this new addition. Little did we know that this filly would become something of a superstar and play an enormous part in our recovery as a family following Carmen's death.

Dad decided soon after we lost Carmen that we should name the filly Carmen. The foals always get a paddock name, and this one was never up for debate. As the filly grew, we were amazed at how similar she was to her namesake; 'high spirited' was how Dad liked to refer to her! Two years after Carmen's accident, it came time to submit Carmen's race names to the Harness Racing Board. We loved doing this with Dad and always had fun trying to come up with smart or simply ridiculous names for the list. The list of names had Dad's first preference at the top—Carmen Leah—Leah being Carmen's middle name. He was thrilled when it came back as her confirmed racing name.

Not long after Carmen Leah's name had been confirmed, we had a family get-together at home with the Millers. Mum's brother, Hughie, and his wife Sandra had four girls—we were all similar in age. We had spent so much time with the Miller girls growing up—

nights at the trots, loads of school holiday swaps, horse trail rides, and memorable outings to the movies! This weekend was significant for another reason. It was the night Dad sat the seven of us girls down and asked if we would like to race Carmen Leah together. Dad had already spent time with Carmen Leah breaking her in, and he was confident that she had enough ability to pay her way. We initially laughed, thinking there would be no way we could afford our own horse. But after some discussion around likely training costs and what we might need to contribute as an initial start-up cost, we were soon confident that we could do it. And with that, Carmen's Racing Syndicate was born.

Dad suggested we give Carmen Leah to a young Bendigo trainer Graham McDermott. He lived not far from where Mum and Dad were and was already training another of Dad's pacers. I'm not sure if Graham knew what he was getting himself into when he accepted Carmen Leah into his stable. Not only did he take on a high-spirited filly with rather bad manners, but he also took on a group of seven young women who would follow him to race meets all over Victoria. Graham had his own little posse!

Carmen Leah's first race was on 20 November 1998, three years and two days after we had lost Carmen. She raced with a key tag attached to her breastplate—inside were two photos of Carmen. Dad had these made up years earlier, and everyone who knew Carmen had one of these on their car keys. Dad described Carmen Leah's first couple of starts as abject failures as she finished close to last. Graham's one-on-one care soon saw a change in her behaviour, and we were hopeful that she might eventually be put in a race where she could finish near the front. Her next couple of races were in the El Dorado series at Moonee Valley, which would see her race against horses who had already earned $100,000 in prize money. She ran eighth in her first heat and last in her second, but we were all pretty happy that she had at least handled herself a little better than in her previous starts.

Carmen Leah's next start was back at Moonee Valley, but this time it was for maiden three-year-olds, a race for three-year-olds that had not yet won a race. It was much easier than her previous couple of races. It was 9 August 1999, and only her fifth start. It was a Monday, so Michelle and I decided to take the day off work and attend the race meeting. Graham was a man of few words, but he was hopeful Carmen Leah would put in a better showing for us, and she didn't disappoint. I'm unsure if a maiden win had ever been met with such joy. Carmen Leah crossed the line in first place, and Michelle and I were jumping, screaming, crying, and hugging each other. In addition to our wild reaction trackside, Carmen Leah connections all over the country were listening in and watching on pay TV. I know there were plenty of tears shed for Carmen that day.

Dad had posted a message on a harness racing web forum a couple of months prior, and the story behind the naming of Carmen Leah had started to spread far and wide. Dad had been responding to posts for months, with the harness racing community wishing us well with our little filly. After Carmen Leah's first win, the web forum exploded with messages from people who had taken an interest in Carmen Leah. Dad spent a fair bit of time replying to posts from strangers all over Australia—she had started to gather quite a following.

Unsurprisingly, the group of young women known as Carmen's Racing Syndicate was starting to get a name for itself too! A group of young women at the trots was a rare sight. At the time of Carmen Leah's first win, the ages of the syndicate members were: Maher girls—Michelle 27, Katrina 25, and Jasmine 23; and the Miller girls—Julie 25, Alison 23, Lisa 21, and Cathy 19.

Around this time, we decided we needed to get some shirts made up. They had Carmen's photo on the front and Carmen's Racing Syndicate printed on the back. The shirts became our standard racing attire and coincided with the period when we started to get a bit of media attention. In August 1999, we had a full-page article in *Harness Racing Weekly*, a Victorian newspaper. The article told readers Carmen Leah's story and why her maiden win had created such a fuss. I remember having a conversation in the tearoom with my colleagues in Horsham about Carmen Leah's win and recall one staff member saying, 'Gee, you must really like gambling. It's just a horse.'

I didn't react. I simply replied, 'She is so much more than "just a horse".'

In September 1999, we were contacted by a writer from the *NSW Harness Racing Gazette*. She had heard about Carmen's story and wanted to write an article for the following issue. We weren't expecting the three-page spread, but to this day, 'Go Carmen Go' is still one of my favourite articles about Carmen Leah and our syndicate.

Articles followed in the *Herald Sun*, *The Bendigo Advertiser*, and *The Ballarat Courier*. We thought we had hit the big time when we received a phone call from *Who Weekly* in late 1999. The *Who Weekly* team travelled to Mum and Dad's home at Longlea, and we had the most fantastic time doing the photo shoot! The photographer took photos of Mum and Dad with Carmen Leah and photos with the syndicate. We were having a ball, but Carmen Leah spent the majority of the time tossing her head around and walking all over us!

We were thrilled to see a two-page spread in the January 2000 issue of *Who Weekly*, with a photo of Carmen Leah front and centre surrounded by the syndicate members in our Carmen's Racing Syndicate shirts. The article was fantastic, particularly the quote from trainer Graham who said that every time he raced Carmen Leah, he could hear us girls yelling and cheering him on from out on the track.

By June 2000, we had decided that we should spend some of our winnings on some new silks for Graham. Dad approached the chief steward at Harness Racing Victoria with the design proposal for the new silks, and thankfully they were cleared. It was the first time in Australian harness racing that silks had been allowed to carry a picture of a person. Carmen Leah was going pretty well at that stage, and we were having some serious fun trackside. Her races became huge events, with family and friends all gathering to cheer her on. From her 10 starts in that winter 2000 campaign, Carmen Leah had already notched up one win, four seconds, and two-thirds. Not only were we having fun, but we also had a horse managing to pay her way in terms of training fees, with a little bit left over. We seemed to have a reason to celebrate on the podium nearly every time she raced.

As the manager of the syndicate, it was my job to keep track of the finances. This meant keeping an eye on Carmen's Racing Syndicate bank account, paying Graham's training fees each month, and arranging other incidentals. One such incidental was the minibus hire! We thought it was appropriate to use syndicate funds to pay for a minibus to take us all to one particular race at Moonee Valley. It was a big race—the $150,000 Sires Stakes Final. Two weeks prior, Carmen Leah raced in the qualifying heat and had to finish in the top four to qualify for the prestigious final. She crossed the line in fourth place. We were jumping, screaming, and generally yahooing with excitement, knowing that we had made it into the final. The group behind us who had actually won the race were somewhat bemused by our reaction, and so too were the pay TV and Channel 31 television audiences who saw us on their screens as the camera operator had assumed by our reaction that we were the winning connections!

The Sires Stakes Final meant Carmen's Racing Syndicate was invited into the boardroom at Moonee Valley racecourse. We had so much fun loading ourselves and our supplies onto the minibus for the trip to Moonee Valley. Hughie agreed to drive, and we sang, danced, and laughed the entire way there. Upon arrival, we made our way to the boardroom to rub shoulders with the VIPs of harness racing. They didn't know what had hit them. We made a grand entrance wearing our customary Carmen's Racing Syndicate shirts, with our partners and friends alongside us. We were ready for a great night, and with meals and drinks supplied, we were all pretty damn excited.

The big moment arrived, and it was time to race. We watched together from the stands and cheered Carmen Leah on to run the best last we have ever seen. We weren't disappointed. We were rapt that she had made the final of such a big race! We made a quick dash to the stalls to thank Graham and congratulate him on such a magnificent last before returning to party on in the boardroom. The night ended with the syndicate members standing on their chairs singing their customary song, 'There's only one Carmen Leah' to the tune of 'There's only one Tony Lockett', while the rest of the boardroom joined in and cheered us on.

I look back on those days, and we had so much fun! Carmen Leah came when the immediate shock and loss of losing Carmen had passed. It was what we needed to get ourselves back up and on the road to recovery. Every time we got together to watch Carmen Leah race, we remembered Carmen and celebrated her life. We would gather at Carmen Leah's stall before the race wishing

Graham good luck, and we would all step in her poo! We had done it accidentally before one of her wins, so we all jumped on board, making it a pre-race ritual. Racegoers would see us and say, 'Here come the Carmen's Racing Syndicate girls.' We had doors opened for us, and well wishes passed on regularly. Everyone knew when we had had a win because we would break into 'there's only one Carmen Leah' in celebration. We were generally happy to sing it anywhere—on the podium, in the bar, and certainly on that minibus!

We were lucky to have had a horse that was so consistent and provided us with so many good times. She had 60 starts over her career with six wins, eight seconds, and nine thirds and earned us $28,200 in the process. We only ever contributed to her account once in that first year. For the rest of it, we just enjoyed the ride.

We all have scrapbooks with Carmen Leah articles and, of course, the winning race photos. We usually managed to get a bit of a discount when ordering seven copies, which usually extended to nine, with Mum and Dad, and Hughie and Sandra, getting copies too.

We raced Carmen Leah together for four years, after which we retired her to Michelle's property at Bungaree. She enjoyed her days being ridden by Michelle and later had several foals of her own. Life was bliss.

The racing days have passed. And although Carmen's Racing Syndicate has formally disbanded, we still reminisce about Carmen. We are now celebrating the 40th birthdays and our own children's birthdays. But those treasured years of racing Carmen Leah remain a favourite time for us all. We know Carmen was with us trackside, cheering, and we had so much fun with her.

That high-spirited filly was so much more than 'just a horse'.

Chapter 11

Ten years

It was 18 November 2005, the 10th anniversary of Carmen's death in her car crash. A lot had happened in those 10 years. Our three girls were all married—Michelle to Tony, Katrina to Simon, and Jasmine to Mark. We sold our beloved house in Longlea and moved to Ballarat to be closer to our children, grandchildren, and extended family.

We had six amazing grandchildren, and it seemed as though our lives revolved around them. We would often be the designated school pick-up. We would take them to their various sports training, and invariably, we would stay and watch them train. Then, of course, we would take them to their respective homes. We were living the ideal life with our families. Living the dream.

Carmen's death was still traumatic. It was painful to think that we lost our beautiful Carmen 10 short years earlier on this day. Our lives had been shattered and irreversibly changed forever.

Where have those 10 years gone?
How is it that the years go by so quickly,
but the days without Carmen seem so long?

I had telephoned my mum the day before to see how she was, and she asked me if I was calling her because it was Carmen's anniversary.

John Maher

> *Mum was a day early,*
> *but after 10 years,*
> *what's in a day?*

It was profound that Mum should make her comment because it magnified the ongoing pain that Carmen's death had brought to everyone. At 78 years of age, my mum shouldn't have had to remember the anniversary of the death of her granddaughter. She should still have been celebrating Carmen's life.

Early that morning, Ange and I made our way to Carmen's tree. We were there at 8:00 am in readiness for our remembrance of Carmen's 8:08 am car crash 10 years earlier. We had not done this for six years, but today was the 10th anniversary—it was special. As at all previous visits, Ange and I held hands, said some prayers for Carmen, and placed flowers and a couple of angels at the base of the tree. We remembered, and we mourned the loss of our beautiful little girl. Poor Carmen.

On this anniversary, I had decided that everyone should get together to celebrate Carmen. I designed a 10th-anniversary invitation and tracked down so many people—many of Carmen's school friends—and we were anticipating a truly memorable day! We booked a function room at a hotel in Bendigo. I knew it would be a good opportunity to reconnect and remember. I also had a surprise organised for everyone. I had spent the month prior collating video footage and photos of Carmen, and I had put them all on a DVD and had a copy for everyone. Of course, Carmen's favourite music played throughout the DVD, which proved to be a huge hit.

Carmen's 10th anniversary was a wonderful celebration of her life, with everyone in the room smiling and happy. It was fantastic to catch up with people we hadn't seen for many years. Seeing so many of Carmen's school friends was brilliant. They made an effort to come, and to me, that proved Carmen had the best friends in the world. Carmen's extended family had also travelled far and wide to support us and each other on that day.

Of course, while it was wonderful to have everyone together, it was also a stark reminder of what could have been for Carmen. Carmen's sisters, cousins, and friends had all started their families. Seeing them with their young children was a reminder that

Carmen had missed out on so much, including having a family of her own.

Throughout the happy day, tears were shed, but not too many, as we shared stories of Carmen. There was much more laughter than tears because we all remembered Carmen for being Carmen. We remembered the funny, silly, crazy, sensitive, goofy, caring, smiling, unique Carmen as we watched her photos scrolling through on the big screen. Carmen had brought everyone together again as she had done when she was alive. And we had a great day.

Everyone talked of the days when, for whatever reason, they were thinking of Carmen. I know when that happens to me, I always take the time to appreciate the moment. I love to be in that moment because memories and feelings come flooding back, and Carmen feels so close.

For many years I dreamed about Carmen often. Dreams where I could see her clearly, and I could hear her voice. Sadly, that almost never happens now, and I miss those dreams and those reminders.

Chapter 12

Twenty years

It was 18 November 2015, and I absolutely could not believe it had been 20 years since we lost Carmen. Although I had come a long way without Carmen, she played a bigger role in my life than I could have ever imagined.

Over the years, I have learned to deal with the shock, grief, and pain following Carmen's death. But still, anger remained.

> *I'm angry that Carmen was killed in that car crash when she was so young and had so much to live for.*
> *I'm angry that when we gather as a family, Carmen is not with us.*
> *I'm angry that I am not a grandfather to her children like I am to the children of Michelle, Katrina, and Jasmine.*
> *I am most angry about the fact that I can't give Carmen a cuddle.*

I reflected on the past 20 years and the impact that losing Carmen had on all of us. I felt especially sad for Michelle, Katrina, and Jasmine because I knew how gut-wrenching that anniversary was for them.

These three girls had Carmen in their lives for 18 years. You can't grow up with your little sister, nurse her, play, argue, cuddle, sleep with, and love your little sister every day for 18 years and not be heartbroken remembering those remarkably good times.

I saw the hurt and despair in their eyes. They didn't have to say anything to me. I could tell by the cuddles they gave me that there was more feeling and the need to hold on for a little bit longer. In private, I was so sad for them because Carmen was the irreplaceable little sister lost. And then, I felt so sad for Ange and myself. And for Carmen. I am never ashamed to cry for Carmen. A good cry never hurt anyone.

Carmen is the irreplaceable little sister lost.

We decided we should spend Carmen's 20th anniversary together and had a wonderful day in Melbourne. It was just Ange, Michelle, Katrina, Jasmine, and me. It was good to get away; even better, we were all together. We thought about Carmen and talked about Carmen, and it was a great day that didn't feel overly sad. I know we were all coping better. Perhaps Mum was right; time was slowly healing us.

Part 4

Carmen's Legacy

Chapter 13

Carmen changing lives

Two years after we lost Carmen, I established my personal road safety presentation for schools in the hope that I could empower students to be safer road users. When a school brings Carmen's Road Safety Message to its students for the first time, you can guarantee that Carmen's story will become a permanent road safety education feature in that school's curriculum. Carmen's Road Safety Message is widely regarded as the best road safety message of its kind.

I wish to acknowledge the amazing schools that have brought Carmen's Road Safety Message to their students because they provide them with valuable life education. I've met and worked with countless outstanding and caring teachers and student welfare coordinators who have their student's best interests at heart. They have welcomed me and Carmen's Road Safety Message with open arms.

I've met many teachers who have suffered the pain of losing a student. Tragically, some have lost several students over their teaching careers. I feel their hurt and loss, which the students don't fully understand. Students see them simply as teachers and educators when in fact, every student unknowingly creates a bond with their teacher. Your teacher is not just a teacher. This is your teacher, and your teacher will always remember you.

I know a teacher who displays photos of four of her past students who lost their lives on the roads—they are on her desk in her home office. Sadly, I've met several teachers who have also lost a child, a parent, or a sibling in a car crash. When they hear Carmen's story, it's difficult for them because those memories come flooding back.

My first love is presenting Carmen's story to schools because the students I share this powerful message with are our future road users. I hope that by arming them with Carmen's Road Safety Message, they will be better prepared for their journey in life, especially on the roads. Carmen's story can save them from senseless road accidents and spare their family and friends from being forced to live the life we live. We live our lives every day without Carmen.

Indeed, we live the life that too many other Australian families are forced to live due to the death of a family member or, tragically, in many cases, the loss of multiple family members in car crashes. Many more families also live with the ongoing impact of injuries. All because of mistakes or poor choices on the road.

Throughout my presentations, I see students laugh, and I see them cry. I also see every student fixated on me and mesmerised by Carmen's story. I know Carmen is touching their hearts, moving them to become the best road users they can be. She even moves them to be better family members and better human beings.

Immediately after my presentations, many students come up and shake my hand. Many more, however, are so moved they give me a cuddle in appreciation of how Carmen has empowered them. They say how sorry they are for us. I tell them not to be sorry because Carmen is still in our lives, and now she's in theirs.

One of my fondest memories since delivering Carmen's story happened after a presentation at a large Melbourne school a few years ago. I'd finished speaking, and many of the students had come to thank me, shake my hand, or give me a hug. One of those students was a tall, burly year 12 student who towered over me. He approached me and smiled, picked me up, and gave me the biggest bear hug of all time. I said, 'Thank you for that. It means a lot that you would do that in front of your peers.'

His reply was, 'I didn't do it for them. I did it for you, your family, and especially Carmen.'

Another memorable experience reinforcing the impact of Carmen's story was in Ballarat after a presentation in 2011. The room had emptied, and I was packing up my computer when two students returned to the room.

Both were crying and asked the principal if they could speak to me. I went over to the girls and asked how I could help them.

One of them asked me, 'How long does this last?'

I responded, 'How long does what last?'

'How long do you miss them for?'

'As you can see, I'm still missing Carmen after 16 years.'

'Yes, I can see that you still miss Carmen.'

Through much sobbing, she shared that her sister, two years older than her, had committed suicide just 14 months earlier. I asked her if she was getting help, and she said yes, she was seeing a counsellor, but she didn't feel it was helping her.

I pointed out to her that although I was not a counsellor, I was experienced in loss. I told her that one of the best things I had done to help me with my feelings of loss was to get a key tag made with Carmen's photo in it.

I took my keys out of my pocket and showed the young girl the key tag dangling among the keys, displaying two photos of Carmen. I told her how our family and many of our friends had these key tags on our car keys, and for us, it made a difference because we could take Carmen with us wherever we went. She leapt forward, hugged me, and told me she would do the same thing.

When I returned to the principal and health nurse, they asked what had happened. I told them about the student's sister and was staggered to find out that neither of them was aware of this student's plight.

There are many students who carry burdens like this, and unfortunately, many of them keep their problems to themselves. This is where presentations like mine can help to open dialogue about tough issues.

At the beginning of every presentation, I let students know that it is okay for them to leave if they find Carmen's story too confronting. Some of the bravest students sit through my presentation crying but refusing to leave because they need to hear Carmen's story. I am touched when I see friends cuddling and supporting each other during or after the presentation. Even the young men, year 10, 11, and 12 students, hug each other and say how much they appreciate them and their friendship.

I am the luckiest member of my family because I speak about Carmen almost every day. This means that Carmen is in my life at that time. It's difficult, at times, to relive Carmen's death in her car crash. There are some days when it feels like Carmen is standing beside me. Those days are the best because I can feel her presence. I know that Carmen empowers these students, and that has an emotional impact on me.

I wish I could adequately express the pride I feel in Carmen when students and adults come up to me after my presentation, hug me or shake my hand, and tell me what Carmen's Road Safety Message has meant to them. And how it has changed their lives by making them think differently about road safety. Students and teachers also tell me that after hearing Carmen's story, they appreciate each family member more and will not hesitate to hug them or tell them how much they love them.

I feel excitement and anticipation when I'm about to present Carmen's Road Safety Message to students at a school. I'm excited about the prospect that Carmen might touch someone's life and influence them to make better decisions as a road user and in life. I believe these students will become leaders amongst their friends after hearing Carmen's story, and I know if that happens, more lives will be saved.

In past years, six schools had to postpone or cancel my presentation because tragedy had struck the school. In the case of one Victorian country school, I was scheduled to present on Friday but received a phone call from the coordinator. This teacher advised me that my presentation would have to be postponed because a student had taken his own life the week earlier. This teacher, who had heard Carmen's story on four previous occasions at the school, also said, 'If only he'd heard Carmen's story last week, he might not have done this.'

And I agree with her.

Sadly, another school postponed because two students were seriously injured after being hit by a car while using the school crossing. A third school had to cancel after a mother and her daughter were killed in a car crash on their way home from school. Yet another school cancelled after an 18-year-old student in year 12 was killed on his motorbike two days before the school holidays ended. Sadly, incidents such as these occur all too frequently.

I watch the road toll closely and know that the most dangerous time for students is during the school holidays. Students are idle, looking for things to do. Some get bored and take risks. This is when some students may be tempted to steal cars, take joy rides, and travel in cars with reckless and dangerous drivers. Some passengers may encourage the normally sensible driver to take risks on the roads because they're looking for a thrill. Invariably, students have been killed by the end of the school holidays, and many more have been seriously injured.

While giving Carmen's road safety presentation, I impress upon students that they are responsible for their actions on the roads. I urge them to understand their life choices, especially on the roads, may determine whether they live or die.

We all know that speed kills, drunk driving kills, taking drugs and driving kills, and that texting or talking on the phone while driving kills. Though not widely known, the first six months after getting their licence is the most dangerous period of every driver's life. But the statistic closest to my heart is that of fatigue because we lost Carmen to fatigue while she was driving. Fatigue is the silent and deadly killer on our roads. Statistics show that 28% of all road deaths are due to fatigue.

Thanks to two young students who heard Carmen's story, Carmen has a Facebook page. The students asked me if they could set up a Facebook page for Carmen because they wanted the world to know how Carmen had changed their lives. I read every comment posted on Carmen's Facebook page and always respond with a comment. I appreciate and love getting comments from students, parents, and teachers. It shows that they have been so moved by the presentation that they were prepared to express their feelings publicly. The original Facebook page has since undergone some changes and is now www.facebook.com/CarmensLegacy/.

The results of delivering Carmen's message at school are incredible. One that sticks fondly in my mind was the magnificent reaction of the Year 11 students at a large girls' college in Brisbane. Of the 212 students who attended the presentation, 129 saw fit to comment on Carmen's Facebook page. This is a measurable result of my presentation and Carmen's true-life story.

With Carmen's message fresh in their mind, students go to Carmen's Facebook page and make their feelings known. They express their personal feelings and make commitments to be safe and to look after their lives for their family and friends. They are saying they're grateful their school brought Carmen into their lives. They understand this is a crucial life lesson, demonstrated in very personal detail.

From a school's perspective, Carmen's Road Safety Message is a critical part of its students' holistic life education, specifically in the critical area of road safety. The Facebook results amplified Carmen's story as it broadcasts to thousands of students, teachers, and parents. This is a quantifiable result for schools, and they can clearly see that Carmen's Road Safety Message has had an impact on their students. It justifies the school's investment in bringing Carmen's message to its community.

I'm proud that Carmen's story has impacted students and schools. The parents of these students should never underestimate what their school has done for their son or daughter in this crucial area of road safety. It is above and beyond the normal curriculum.

The feedback I receive from so many of the students, teachers, and parents helps to drive me forward and fuels my desire to make a difference in their lives. At the end of this book, you'll find a small selection of the thousands of Facebook comments and direct messages I've received over the years.

Many parents ask if I have a recording of Carmen's Road Safety Message. I'm delighted to respond that, thanks to the support of St. Joseph's College in Geelong, which allowed me to film my presentation at their school, it is available on DVD.

I believe if every family in Australia watched Carmen's Road Safety Message on DVD or read Carmen's Legacy, we would slash the road toll. I cannot think of a better gift for a learner driver. It could be the gift of life!

I also receive feedback from parents about Carmen's Road Safety Message. One phone call from an appreciative mum gives the perfect example. She told me that her son played under 18 football and, as he wasn't yet 18, a teammate and friend picked him up every Saturday morning and took him to football. This friend and teammate delighted in squealing his tyres up the road as he left every Saturday morning. He knew it upset his mum, but he continued to do it, and she was worried for her son's safety. She purchased Carmen's DVD and sat her children down to watch Carmen's story together as a family. She then asked her son to invite his friend and teammate to pick him up 60 minutes earlier the next Saturday morning, which he did. She made her son and his friend sit down and watch Carmen's Road Safety Message and added that her daughter got out of bed to watch it again. When it was finished, the friend thanked her and said, 'Thank you, that was amazing, and you may have saved my life.' The mum explained her reply was, 'I'm so pleased. But to be honest, I was more worried and concerned with saving my son's life.'

Chapter 14

Supporting Carmen's Road Safety Message

On 20 October 2017, I brought Carmen's story into the lives of the attendees at the Bendigo and Adelaide Bank Conference in Victoria.

Ange, Michelle, Katrina, and Jasmine were invited and proudly attended. I guess I'm used to the reactions I receive when bringing our true-life story to organisations. This one didn't seem to be any different, with laughter and a few tears, followed by lots of cuddles, comments, and conversations.

However, the Bendigo and Adelaide Bank proved how different a community bank really is. It put the wheels in motion for me to bring Carmen's Road Safety Message to the many communities served by Bendigo Bank community branches.

Thanks to the generosity of the Bendigo and Adelaide Bank, and its determination to keep its members, customers, and communities safe, I embarked on a journey that saw Carmen's story impact and empower entire communities, sporting clubs, and secondary schools under the umbrella of the Bendigo Bank community branches.

One of those community bank branches, the Mount Beauty and District Community Bank, was so moved by Carmen's story and how it had impacted the secondary college students and the attendees at the community presentation that the branch manager, Shelley, invited me to return the following week. Shelley asked if I could bring Ange as the Mount Beauty and District Community Bank Board members would like to meet with us.

We were in for a *huge* surprise on our return. Shelley had informed the Board that my 2009 Subaru Forester had 383,000 kilometres on the clock. To our amazement, the Mount Beauty and District Community Bank Board offered to sponsor us with a new Subaru Forester. The Board members wanted to make certain I continued to take Carmen's Road Safety Message and education reliably and safely as I travelled the roads.

Only a month earlier, I had discussed with Ange how concerned I was that my car might let me down while travelling to a presentation. Perhaps Carmen was watching over us and moved the Board members to such generosity.

My family and I are so grateful for the support of the Mount Beauty and District Community Bank because I now travel to my presentations in my new Subaru Forester. It is the safest and best vehicle I've ever driven. I am proud to drive my Subaru, complete with Carmen's Road Safety, including Carmen's photo, and the Mount Beauty and District Community Bank emblazoned on the side of the car. Everyone knows this is Carmen's Road Safety Message vehicle.

Recently, the generosity of a Warrnambool family impacted by road tragedy thought of Carmen's Road Safety at their most tragic moment. On 27 August 2021, I was emailing a school that, like so many schools, was forced to cancel my presentation due to COVID restrictions when I was interrupted by a phone call from Warrnambool College. The College had rescheduled my 2021 presentation on two separate occasions due to COVID.

This call, however, was to be so different. The Business Manager, Chris, informed me that a year 10 student had lost his life in a car crash the previous day. I had received many such phone calls over the 24 years of bringing Carmen's Road Safety Message to schools. I am never prepared for such a call, nor am I prepared for my emotional reaction because these are my schools, and we are connected. These schools allow me to work with them to educate their students in the critical area of safe road use.

Chris informed me that the parents of Joel, the year 10 student who lost his life in a car accident the previous day, had arrived at Warrnambool College at 8:30 am that morning. Joel's family asked the school to inform everyone they would like donations to be made to Carmen's Road Safety instead of flowers.

I was shocked, and my lack of response caused Chris to ask me if I would like to take a minute. She could tell I was emotional from the start when told they had lost a student, and now, with this news, I needed time. Thoughts flashed through my mind of this devastated family making such a request within hours of losing their son in a car crash.

She continued by explaining the family had come to this decision following a request by their daughter, Hannah, who had heard Carmen's Road Safety Message just two years earlier when she was in year 10 (now in year 12). Hannah asked her parents if they could support Carmen's Road Safety instead of buying flowers. In their darkest hour, this incredible family supported Carmen's story in the hope it could stop another family from experiencing the loss and pain they were now experiencing.

My diary was open on my desk while I was speaking, and I was staring in disbelief at the date, 26 August. It was just two days after that date I was to have presented at Warrnambool College, but COVID intervened. Life can be so cruel. Joel would have heard Carmen's story had it not been for the COVID lockdown.

A GoFundMe page was set up for Carmen's Road Safety, and funds flooded in. Through the comments attached to donations, I soon learned how respected Joel and his family were. I immediately knew he was a special young man.

Ange and I have since met Greg, Jo, Hannah, and Bonnie, Joel's family. I was delighted to learn from Hannah that after she heard Carmen's story in 2019, she was one of many students who gave me a cuddle.

Ange and I attended the beautiful celebration of Joel's life at his online funeral. I sincerely thank Joel's family and everyone who donated to Carmen's Road Safety in memory of Joel.

Their actions inspired me to record Carmen's Road Safety as a webinar. Thanks to the donations received, I provided it to every secondary school in Victoria at no fee. I then sent it to every secondary school in Australia, and Joel will continue to play a significant role in Carmen's story and the lives of thousands of students.

Like our family, Joel's family ask that you share their message with your friends. What happened to them can happen to any family, even yours. We don't want another family to feel the pain of road trauma.

We hear about road trauma every day. It is always someone else's story until it becomes your story.

I was to learn that there was so much more to the tragic loss of Joel in that car crash in Warrnambool. A 19-year-old female also lost her life, and a 17-year-old female was critically injured and flown to Melbourne. Two occupants of the car had also attended Warrnambool College, and all three worked at the Warrnambool McDonald's store.

Within two weeks, I was contacted by Monique, the manager for the company that owns 12 McDonald's stores, including the Warrnambool McDonald's store. The critical injuries of one, plus the deaths of two of its employees, sent shockwaves through their stores—employees at the Warrnambool store were shattered.

In discussions with Monique, we decided I would produce a specific 'Carmen's Road Safety – McDonald's' recorded webinar for their stores, in which they have 1,600 employees. This would be a particularly sensitive presentation because I know that most McDonald's employees are in a similar age bracket to Joel.

McDonald's has played the presentation 57 times, so I'm confident that Carmen and Joel have greatly impacted all 1,600 employees and management. I thank Anthony and Monique for allowing me to support them as they bring road safety and a path forward for everyone impacted by these tragedies.

The loss of two lives in this Warrnambool car crash clearly shows how many people were devastated and affected: the families of the deceased; first responders; extended families and friends; schools; teachers and their families; students and their families; communities; Warrnambool McDonald's stores; eleven more McDonald's stores; Carmen's Road Safety, yes, me; and the list goes on, and on, and on.

Chapter 15

Dad's a legend

Written by Katrina

Many people feel pride when they think of their family and the achievements that their loved ones have made throughout their lives. I, however, count myself lucky to be in that special category where pride doesn't even begin to scratch the surface. I often reflect on the adversity my dad has faced, the mental and physical challenges he has endured, and the incredible strength it has taken to overcome these obstacles. My heart swells with admiration and awe at the resilience and determination of this amazing man.

When Dad was injured in his car accident, the scars were more than skin-deep. He had numerous physical injuries from which to recover, along with a frontal lobe brain injury, and probably the most difficult of all, the mental scars from his accident where a bright young girl tragically lost her life. Whilst struggling with these burdens, being told—at 42 years of age and with a family depending on him—that he would never work again was a huge blow for Dad. To his credit, Dad always remained positive and hopeful that we would somehow get through it together.

I'm sure it wasn't always this way behind closed doors or in the dead of night, but Mum and Dad always presented a strong and united front to us girls who sometimes wondered what the future would hold for us, knowing Dad was unable to work.

As we were adjusting to our new way of life, and let's face it, our 'new dad', we were dealt the cruellest of blows when our beloved, sweet little sister Carmen was taken from us. It shattered our lives in a way that cannot be put into words and cannot be imagined unless you have experienced such devastation first-hand. Thankfully we had the one thing that would get us through such a horrific experience—each other.

For all of us, the next couple of years passed in a haze of depression, disbelief, grief, sadness, and fear. Despite that, we loved and supported each other as best we could and helped each other through those dark times. Dad often talks about how his mum, Morney, was responsible for instilling strong family values. This fierce sense of family, togetherness, and camaraderie kept us going and enabled us to support each other even though we suffered so much as individuals. We relied on the love of our family and friends and the precious memories of Carmen to get us through that terrible time.

As the rest of us struggled with our internal battles to accept what happened to our dear Carmen and attempted to adjust to life without her, Dad, incredibly, managed to turn his attention outward. Two years after Carmen's death, four teenagers lost their lives in a horrific car accident near Bendigo. This event became a catalyst for change in Dad. He asked, 'Why are so many young people losing their lives on our roads?' And crucially, 'Is there anything I can do to stop it?'

In asking these questions, Dad began the incredible journey of transforming himself from a victim of road trauma to one of Australia's leading educators on road safety. Instead of wallowing in sadness and self-pity like many would have done in Dad's circumstances, he became proactive in trying to tackle the very thing that had taken so much from him.

From humble beginnings presenting at just a few secondary schools a year, Dad's road safety presentation 'Carmen's Road Safety Message' now reaches around 70 schools and 13,000 students every year, along with attendees at many community, sporting, and corporate events around Australia and internationally.

As a family, we attend one of Dad's presentations nearly every year. This is our way of supporting Dad and showing him how proud we are of him. I will be totally honest, though, and tell you that I find the experience extremely harrowing. Listening to Dad recount his own accident and then explain to students how we lost Carmen, and the effect that had and continues to have on our family breaks my heart all over again. But as I sit there sobbing through the presentation, I ask myself the same question over and over: How can Dad put himself through this day in, day out, year after year?

The answer, of course, is that he does it for the children. He does it for their families and friends, so they won't have to experience the hurt and suffering we have endured. And you only have to look around at the students or read their comments on Carmen's Facebook page to know that Dad's presentation has truly and irrevocably impacted their lives. I sometimes wonder how many young lives Dad has saved or how many horrific injuries have been avoided because a young person decided not to take a risk as a result of hearing Dad's talk.

Another amazing outcome from Dad's talk is that it doesn't just speak to young people about road safety. These young adults take so much more than that from Dad's presentation. After hearing Dad speak, many students have been inspired to reassess their lives and actions, whether that was regarding excessive drinking, drug use, self-harm, or participating in a myriad of other risk-taking behaviours.

Many students have been moved to reach out and reconnect with their families and loved ones after hearing Carmen's story. Dad has received countless emails from parents and guardians informing him that their son or daughter came home after hearing his talk and told them how much they loved and appreciated them, vowing that they would treat their life as the precious gift that it is. Students often apologised to their parents for being distant and making bad choices. Dad's presentation provides a fantastic opportunity for parents to sit down and have a frank and open discussion with their teenagers.

I cannot count the number of times I have been stopped on the street, at work, or at school pick-up, by someone who has heard

Dad's presentation. Friends I have known for many years will say things like, 'I had no idea.' 'Your poor family. How did you get through that?' 'How does your dad keep reliving it?' 'Your dad is amazing. I can't say thank you enough.' 'Please thank your dad for keeping our kids safe.'

People have often approached me with stories about the profound effect that Dad's presentation has had on them or their children. I was once told that a student had heard Dad's presentation and had been so moved that he went home that night and confessed to his parents that he had been planning on taking his own life. It wasn't until he had heard Dad speak that he realised what this would do to his parents, siblings, family, and friends. Armed with this knowledge, he confided in his parents and asked them to get him the help he needed. Another life was saved. And another reason to be proud of my dad.

In dedicating his life to bringing Carmen's Road Safety Message into the lives of young people, Dad is satisfied and fulfilled knowing that he is making a difference. I see how thrilled Dad is when he receives positive feedback through the amazing messages on Carmen's Facebook page, via email, on the phone, and in person. And for Dad, I know that would be enough. I am, however, proud to say that Dad's presentation has brought him much public recognition, and rightly so.

Dad was nominated for the National Australia Day Council's Australian of the Year Award in 2013, 2014, 2015, and 2017.

On 4 December 2015, he was named the CommBank Australian of the Day.

In 2014 Carmen's Road Safety won the Victorian Regional Achievement and Community Award in the VACC-sponsored SAFETY category. It was an enormous accolade for Dad. As a family, we went to Etihad Stadium. We watched with tears in our eyes as Dad received a standing ovation while being recognised for his tireless work spreading Carmen's road safety message to the youth of Australia.

In 2015, Carmen's Road Safety won the City of Ballarat Community Safety Award in the Road Safety category. It was fantastic to see our local council recognise the amazing work that Dad does in the Ballarat community.

I know Dad doesn't do any of this for awards or recognition, but I think it is wonderful to see his work recognised in public forums. He works extremely hard, often at great personal cost, for the benefit of others, and I believe he deserves every accolade he receives.

All forms of media seek Dad out for his thoughts and input on the ongoing challenges our nation faces with the road toll. He has been a guest on Kerri-Anne Kennerley's morning show, numerous news and current affairs programs, and podcasts and has been interviewed by many newspapers. We often receive a family group text message informing us that Dad will be interviewed on the radio in 15 minutes so that we can all tune in.

Whenever I listen to Dad being interviewed, I inevitably find myself in tears. And I know that Mum, Michelle, and Jasmine feel the same way because no matter where we are and what we are doing, we are forever connected by the loss of Carmen. Over 25 years have passed, yet we still hurt and cry for Carmen. We are eternally thankful, however, that she is still part of our lives through the work that Dad is doing, and we have come to embrace the fact that Dad's work is Carmen's legacy.

Chapter 16

Carmen's life lessons

In losing Carmen, I learned some of the most valuable life lessons.

I learned that we were fortunate to have had Carmen in our lives for 18 years and three months, and yes, those three months were so important.

It wasn't until we lost Carmen that I truly understood her amazing gift to us and how she impacted and enriched our lives daily.

I learned that you should never give a cuddle away cheaply. I now give cuddles with more meaning and affection because I know how valuable and precious they are. If I could cuddle Carmen today, I would never let her go!

Every time we see our girls and grandchildren, there are cuddles all around.

I had always told my children I loved them, but on that fateful Saturday morning when we lost Carmen, I didn't get to tell her how much I loved her.

I learned that I should repeatedly tell those dear to me that I love them.

After her passing, Carmen empowered me to take back control of my life. And she became the subject—and the catalyst—for my desire to help people understand how important they are. I needed Carmen's story to become a lesson for others.

Losing Carmen taught me how fragile life could be. She showed me that things happen in our lives that are beyond our control, and no matter what the event or how difficult the challenge, it is how we respond that will determine who we are and where we end up in life.

Carmen taught me that we all have a choice. You may allow yourself to be engulfed by sadness, hurt, anger, or the many negative responses available, which will change you as a person, ultimately making your life miserable. Or you can choose to respond positively with power and determination, and that will change you as a person because you will remember and cherish the good times. You may even choose to celebrate the event by turning it into a positive, as I have.

Losing Carmen taught me never to underestimate my children, as I had underestimated Carmen. For 18 years and three months, I thought Carmen was just our beautiful youngest child. But she was so much more than that. In her short time on this earth, she had touched our lives so deeply; and had touched so many more lives of which I was unaware.

I'm still stunned by and proud of the number of people who came to pay their respects to Carmen at her funeral. My heart swells with pride for who Carmen was, with how selfless and caring she was towards others. I will never again underestimate my children or my grandchildren!

One of the most powerful lessons for me has been accepting and acknowledging that Carmen is at work through me. I will never undervalue her power to impact the lives of others. When people embrace Carmen's story, the life lessons make them better and more complete people. Because of Carmen, I am a better person, but my life is not yet complete because our work together is not yet done!

Through Carmen, I have learned how strong and valuable a friendship can be. Carmen's friends have shown me the true bond of real friends. They are in contact with us constantly, and they embody Carmen's story.

It was such an incredibly tough and traumatic time. Carmen's friends were all 17 and 18-year-olds. It shows how strong those friendships were because Carmen is still a part of their lives today.

Carmen empowered me to help others. I'm passionate about taking Carmen's Road Safety Message to our youth, knowing that it is students in years 10, 11, and 12 who are learning to drive. I educate them to be cautious, courteous, and conscientious road users.

These young men and women are the future of safety on the roads. They can change the current culture of apathy and the 'it'll never happen to me' attitude. We need our education system to become involved so our future—road safety educated—generations can lead us to safer roads. Education is the key!

Losing Carmen made me acutely aware that fatigue is the silent and deadly killer on our roads. Her death taught me that the instant I start to feel tired when driving, I must stop immediately.

I admit that I used to drive my car when tired. I would push myself to get to my destination. *NEVER AGAIN*. Fatigue is a killer, and I cannot do to my family what Carmen did to us.

Carmen enabled me to put processes in place to combat fatigue. If I become fatigued when driving, I stop immediately in a safe place. I set the alarm on my phone for 15 or 30 minutes, and I have a power nap. I am fortunate because I often go straight to sleep.

I urge everyone to put this practice in place because even if you do not sleep, you're still taking a break. The key to the total success of my strategy is when I wake. I get out of the car and go for a brisk walk for at least 100 metres to get fresh air into my lungs and get the adrenalin pumping. By doing that, I ensure I'm fully awake, and only then will I continue my journey.

When I continue my journey, I am a safer driver for myself, for every other road user, and most importantly, for the people who love me so much, my family.

The loss of Carmen has made me more aware of my responsibility as a driver. If I have passengers in the car, I understand that I am 100% responsible for their lives and my own. I treat the life of every passenger in my car as if it were one of my grandchildren, whose lives I would protect with my own.

I have become a very patient and tolerant driver. I'm aware of the shortcomings of other drivers and, for that matter, all forms of road users. I'm watchful of pedestrians and bike riders, especially those who wear earphones. I'm convinced they are not concentrating completely on the task at hand and can therefore be unpredictable.

I didn't understand that Carmen was the most important person in the world. And you must understand who you are.

YOU are the most important person in the world to the people who love you, and you cannot do to them what Carmen has done to us.

I have learned that there is nothing more powerful than the love of family.

I have learned that you should never be too proud or stubborn to accept help when you need it—embrace it and be thankful.

I have learned that a car crash is not just a car crash.

Chapter 17

Those left behind are the true casualties

When I read or hear about a fatal car crash, I never just see that someone has been killed. I see a family devastated, holding each other and crying. I see a family member pulling themselves away, retreating to a bedroom or the bathroom, where they can cry and cry and cry in private.

I see a family bonded by tragedy. I see a family the next morning at the crash site placing flowers and spending solemn, quiet time, remembering, praying, crying, and supporting each other in their shared grief. I see a family picking out a cemetery plot. I see a family meeting with the priest and arranging a funeral. I see a family at the funeral home selecting a coffin, picking out the colour of the wood, the silk insert, the cross that will sit atop the lid, and the screws that will secure the lid onto the coffin, which will house their beloved family member's body.

I see the family members visiting the doctor, asking for sleeping pills because they can't get to sleep at night because of the thoughts racing through their minds.

No, I don't just see a fatality in that car crash. I see so much more because the true tragedy is the effect on the family and friends who are left behind.

I see my family in their family. I see that family embarking on my family's journey—a life without their loved one. They are just starting on the journey my family has been on for 25 years.

Carmen didn't mean to do this to us, and you will not mean to do it to your loved ones. But if you do, your family's journey from that day onwards will be without the hope of ever giving you that cuddle they so desperately need from you.

As a driver, it is your choice and your decision. We see many car accidents where a passenger has been killed, but the driver survived. So often, in those cases, it has been proven that the driver was under-age, unlicensed, had a blood alcohol content over .05, was affected by drugs, had stolen the car, was hooning or street racing, speeding, or doing one of the many other risky things a driver can do. In most of these cases, the passenger would, or perhaps should have been, aware of the driver's condition or state of mind. Far too often, the passenger supports or encourages risk-taking, which may soon cost them their life.

A critical lesson is to be learned from these accidents. Everyone is 100% responsible for their choices, and choices have consequences.

There is an alarming trend toward people not wearing seat belts. I am staggered because the first thing I do is put on my seatbelt. Can I urge you to please wear your seat belt? It may save your life.

These life-or-death decisions are yours to make. They are played out tens of thousands of times a day. We would significantly reduce the road toll if everyone made the correct, safe decision.

A car crash may be the most violent experience you will ever have, and whether you live or die in that car crash may come down to luck.

Epilogue

Our Lives Today

Every life is precious, and you must understand who you are. You are the most important person in the world to those who love you. You are unique, and you can never be replaced.

It has been more than 25 years since we lost our beautiful Carmen, and we all still use her one-liners, such as,

'It'll be alright!'

'Maysenwell.' Translation: may as well.

'I love you, Carmen Maher. I love you, John Maher.'

Today our lives are as perfect as you can get, minus Carmen. Ange and I are now more commonly known as Mumma and Pa, and we both turned 71 in 2021! Our children have provided us with three magnificent families. Michelle, Tony, and their children Jaida (19) and Ruben (17). Katrina, Simon, and their children Cadell (19) and Lucas (15). Jasmine, Mark, and their children Max (17) and Tess (14).

Parents hope their children will meet and marry someone worthy of them, someone who will love and look after them. We hit the jackpot three times with Tony, Simon, and Mark because they are perfect. And yes, I cuddle my sons-in-law.

I often see Carmen in our two granddaughters, Jaida and Tess. When I see Carmen's expressions in them or hear a typical Carmen comment, I appreciate and savour the moment. And at that time, the granddaughter responsible always gets a HUGE cuddle.

Our grandchildren are the highlights of our lives. They keep us young, and we always pick them up or drop them off somewhere when their parents are too busy, and we love it! Each of them, in their own way, is taking us on their life journey, and they keep us involved.

Although we faced a huge struggle when we lost Carmen, we have been through that and are happy. We understand and appreciate that our family and close friends complete our happiness today as we continue to move forward in life.

Unfortunately, our family is not unique. Too many lives are lost on the roads, and hearts are broken forever through these tragedies.

We can make a difference, and we must make a difference. Take responsibility for your safety as a road user. Own your decision-making, and **you will make a difference**.

I wanted so desperately to tell my story, our story, and why wouldn't I? I thought it would be easily done. After all, I present Carmen's story at more than one hundred school and corporate events every year. I speak about Carmen and my family almost every day. How hard could it be to write it in book form?

At times it seemed I was destined to never complete this book. I found it so difficult getting through Part 2, where I had to relive losing Carmen. I found the written word to be so confronting. It meant I had to go through Carmen's car crash one word at a time, and those words seemed to linger. They became more powerful, emotional, and haunting in my mind, so I often faltered. As I relived everything, it made me cry as if my heart was breaking all over again. And I cried a lot. So much so that I often had to stop typing because I couldn't see the keyboard or screen through my tears. Thankfully, I was always alone when this happened as I needed to be alone.

I completely underestimated how hard writing this book would be. Not just for me, but for the girls and Ange as well. We came together several times at various stages of my draft, and those days were tough. The girls would take turns reading aloud while we all cried our way through the pages. When it got too much, we would take a break, have a coffee, and reconvene with a new reader at the helm. There were times when I would get frustrated the girls hadn't got back to me with their comments on a draft, but of course, that was because they were juggling young families and busy schedules. Sitting down to cry their way through this book wasn't high on their to-do list.

They all wanted me to finish, and I desperately wanted to tell our story. I wanted the world to know how wonderful my family is, and I needed to tell everyone about Carmen! And in doing so, I hope, more than anything, that her story in this written form touches people as deeply as it does when I give my presentations in person.

If this book can bring comfort to a reader who has lost a family member in tragic circumstances, I will be so pleased. I hope it gives you the courage to find your purpose in life with your loved one in your heart.

If it can bring family members closer by allowing every member of the family to understand the wonderful gift they are and how they complete and add to their family, then I will be thrilled.

If this book makes people realise they are beautiful, unique, and important individuals, who have indelibly changed the lives of others and will be forever missed by their loved ones if they were no longer around, it will have been worth the effort.

If one student who hears Carmen's story makes a conscious decision to be the safest driver they can be, my work will have been successful, and a life may have been saved.

If one business brings Carmen's Road Safety Message into the lives of its employees, and those employees fully understand they must get home to their family every day after work, then Carmen has kept a family together.

If every school had this book in the school library, Carmen might touch the lives of more young students, and it may save even more lives.

If the reader of this book gives it to someone they care about as a gift, with the express purpose of seeing them safe on the road, that would be a great compliment.

I would love to see Carmen's story shared with as many people as possible. That is how we can all make sure that Carmen's Legacy lives on. I hope this true-life story has moved you enough to consider purchasing a copy for your loved ones or a copy for someone you care about. Of course, if you give this book as a gift, it should be presented with a warm cuddle.

Imagine if every learner driver received a copy of Carmen's Legacy as a gift. It may empower them to better understand their role as a road user and family member.

Thank you for allowing our family into your lives. Stay safe always. After all, you are the most important person in the world.

On behalf of Ange, Michelle, Katrina, Jasmine, and myself, Carmen is our gift to you.

I love you, Carmen Maher.
You are the most important person in the world.
I miss your cuddles, but I know you are in my life every day.

Acknowledgements

I would like to express gratitude to my family, who have put up with me as I struggled, rode the emotional roller-coaster, but ultimately persevered in writing this book over the past 20 years. For encouraging me to continue even though we all knew I was not a writer and could not write a book. For supporting me when I hit the wall and couldn't go on because of the tears. Thank you all for the amazing times we all shared critiquing the book and making those changes, using boxes of tissues as we all cried through the tough chapters together.

I am so proud we are all in this together as a family. I am thankful that Michelle, Katrina, and Jasmine were so brave and contributed a chapter each. They have added tremendously to the book.

Ange, I understand how you couldn't write a chapter because it would have broken your heart all over again. I know you didn't want me to write this book because you knew how hard it would be on everyone. But you understand why I had to do this and thank you for supporting what we can all be so proud of—Carmen's Legacy.

To my extended family and friends who supported my family and me through the good times and the bad, your selfless support ensured we were never alone.

To every schoolteacher and student I have shared Carmen's story with over the past two decades, all 450,000 of you, thank you. You embraced me, my family, and Carmen, and gave us hope. The feedback I have received from so many of you confirms that what I am doing is appreciated and of value.

To corporate Australia, you have been integral in furthering Carmen's message and ultimately safe road use at your workplace. We have made a difference through our collaboration and may have saved lives. You know your employees are safer road users because, through Carmen's story, you have empowered them to arrive home safely to their families every day after work.

John Maher

Thank you to Mandy Del Vecchio, who helped turn my writings into a book. For you to edit a manuscript written about one of your best friends, Carmen, I know, was heartbreaking for you. I am so pleased you were the one to edit my work because you are very much a part of Carmen's Legacy.

Thank you to Karen Guest, who completed the final edit of my book. Your knowledge, guidance, and wisdom in providing formatting and grammatical changes without affecting the storyline added the polish and professionalism worthy of a book that is so important to my family. You embraced our family through the book and completed a personal edit of Carmen's Legacy; we now have the Second Edition, which is worthy of adding to every reader's library.

About the author

John Maher is an international keynote speaker on road safety, risk, and family. John has been recognised at the community, state, and national levels for bringing Carmen's Road Safety Message to the public. His nominations and awards include:

- Nominated: National Australia Day Council's Australian of the Year Award (2013, 2014, 2015, 2017).
- Winner: Victorian Regional Achievement and Community Awards in the SAFETY category (2014).
- Winner: Ballarat Safe City Award in Road Safety (2015).
- Named: CommBank Australian of the Day (4 December 2015).
- Winner: 2022 City Of Ballarat Youth Awards, Influential Adult – Worker.

Speaking topics
John weaves his true-life tale, engaging audiences of all ages and backgrounds. Carmen's Road Safety Message has been recognised in all forms of media and through schools and corporate organisations in Australia, New Zealand, and Internationally.

Carmen's Road Safety Message
Audience: Secondary schools
Topic: Road safety

John uses the story of his daughter's death in a car accident to educate young drivers on safe road use. This presentation is widely considered the best road safety message you will ever hear. It could save your life or the life of someone you love.

You Never Know What's Around the Corner
Audience: Banking, insurance, corporate
Topic: Road safety and risk protection

John was a successful insurance company manager in country Victoria. He can speak with authority on the life-changing challenges he and his family faced after he was involved in a car crash. Suffering serious injuries, at just 42 years old, John was told he would never work again. John has since become a champion for road safety. His inspirational keynote presentation is sought after across all business sectors, nationally and internationally.

Cuddle Your Kids Forever
Audience: Family
Theme: Motivational and inspirational

In this inspirational talk, John lets the audience into his fragile life, lifts their spirits, and reminds them how precious family and life are. His true-life story inspires families to be the best they can be.

Your Club, Your Responsibility
Audience: Sporting clubs
Topic: Road safety and responsibility

Being involved in sporting clubs since junior football and cricket, John understands the importance of friendship, camaraderie and competition, and the role that every member and supporter plays in a sporting club.

Over his sporting life, John has lost 11 teammates on the roads. Speed, alcohol, fatigue, and inattention have contributed to several of those deaths. Every club has responsibilities to its members, and every member has a responsibility to their club.

We have one life only, and we must look out for each other.

Facebook comments from students and schools

Below is a small selection of the thousands of messages I've received via social media following my presentations in Australian schools. I am honoured to receive such commendations and expressions of appreciation from these amazing Australians. I know Carmen is touching hearts from the grave. These future road users respond magnificently.
Names and school names have been withheld for privacy.

Student
Thank you so much for coming to my school today. It was the most touching presentation I've ever seen and touched my heart very much. I was close to losing my brother in a car crash (like I said today), and it has opened my eyes so much to how I could have lost him. So, after school, I went home and gave my mum and dad a huge hug, texted my brother and told him how much I loved him. Thank you again for coming to talk to us, and may Carmen forever be in our hearts. I will make sure I never drive while tired.

Student
I am in year 11 at *** College. The talk we had today had a serious effect on me. I've been diagnosed with depression and struggle quite a lot. Your talk made me realise how fragile life can be and made me so grateful for the people I have in my life. I know your speech had nothing to do with mental illness, but I made that connection. And I wanted to thank you because I will hold what you said with me forever. Thank you so much for your time; you really helped me.

Student
Hey, I'm a student from Bendigo. I said it while you were there, but it was kind of rushed, and I wanted to make myself a little clearer. I really, really appreciate that you came to our school and told us not just about your own accident, but your daughters too. I can't even begin to imagine how difficult that would be.

Your story really touched me, not just because it's something that is real and is happening all over the world every day, or how passionately you spoke about it. I genuinely feel that you changed my life for the better today, and I want to thank you. I've recently been struggling with my personality, which has led to (quite unfortunately) depression.

I'd been seriously considering suicide until today. When you talked about how you went to counselling and then about how the death of your daughter affected everyone around her, it made me realise how selfish and unfair it would be for me to take my own life. I have to thank you for that.

Student

Being able to hear your story and what you have been through was truly an eye-opener. I was just moved by everything; sitting there today and listening really touched everyone's hearts. I just got my licence a few months ago, and now, after hearing you, I'll always think of Carmen and the impact it has on everyone else. Thank you so much for coming to my school and talking to us today. As soon as I got home, I hugged and told everyone I loved them, even my dad, who didn't know what to do lol. Life puts you down and gives you a reason to stand back up and fight.

Student

I'd just like to say thank you, you presented Carmen's message to a group of my peers at our college. After your presentation, many of my friends' bad driving habits were broken almost instantaneously. I honestly believe, were it not for your presentation, some of them may not be by my side today.

Student

Just want to say a huge thank you! I'm a teen who's been on the verge of suicide for a while now, and your presentation, although not the same, made me think a lot. Realising that I am important and how many people would be affected and how devastated they would be. I know it is road safety, not suicide message, but you have changed my outlook on life, and I won't have those dark thoughts ever again. Thank you!

Teacher

Wow, that is amazing. I have just sent your email to the staff, who are soooo excited!! Had a great talk with the driver's ed students today and was amazed by what they took away from your presentation.

The details and the message they received and remembered were impressive. Please know that Carmen's message has and will continue to touch our school. Both teachers and students are grateful that you take the time to talk so passionately and honestly about subjects most would shy away from.

A funny story for you: our health nurse placed herself behind two troublesome students, ready to intervene if necessary, and she told the staff she did not have to move a muscle as they were so engaged and interested in your story, to which the staff was very impressed! Wishing they could be like that in every class!

Parent

My daughter attended your presentation. My eyes welled with tears as we drove home from school today, with my daughter at the wheel as a learner driver, relaying your heartbreaking story to me. She and I were both impacted by your compelling message.

We can raise our children to become good citizens, but I feel that we lose control of the ability to protect them once they start driving. It's comforting to know that people like yourself are making a difference in the way our children behave when getting behind the wheel. Thank you from the bottom of my heart.

Student

To be completely honest with you, I could not help but try to empathise with you whilst you were explaining Carmen's story. I felt your heartbreak, I felt your sadness, but most definitely, I could see in your eyes how, as a father, you longed for your daughter and missed her dearly.

I cannot imagine how traumatising and saddening it is to lose one of God's gifts to you. I can tell you, without any hesitation, that Carmen was an angel. She was beautiful, and I could tell by the pictures you showed us she was a girl full of life, sincerity, and joy.

Your daughter Carmen is looking over you and your family and is most definitely feeling proud of her father. I am a changed person today. You managed to get down to the very bottom of my heart and evoke my sensitive and personal reaction. You are a gifted man John. To be able to tell Carmen's story to so many people is a gift. It's a gift because it expresses your strength, courage and sincerity. It is people like you who change lives and tattoo a mark on someone forever. I hope God watches over you and your family and makes it somewhat easier for you each day that goes by.

Your angel is looking down on you and smiling each time. She is a proud daughter. I wish I could meet Carmen. Looking at her pictures made me think that *I would've definitely been friends with her* because of her soft heart you expressed and her wonderful nature. I think it's absolutely superb how you go out of your own free will and seek to assist young people in real-life situations that can happen. Your story was unique, and it certainly was one that I will be sharing with many people. God bless you, John, and may you receive endless amounts of happiness and joy in your life. That wish is also for your three daughters, wife, and grandchildren.

Student

Thank you for sharing your road safety story with us! If I ever have a daughter, I will name her Carmen; she seemed amazing.

Connect with John

Please reach out if you want to connect with John, follow Carmen's Road Safety campaign, or book John to speak at your school or business.

www.carmen.com.au

www.facebook.com/CarmensLegacy

carmenroadsafety@gmail.com

Seeking help

If you need help or someone you love needs help, remember, you are not alone. There is always someone who can help. Your doctor is always a good starting point.

Below is a non-exhaustive list of resources you can connect with in your time of need. Provision of this information is not an endorsement of the service. It is intended as a reference for you to start with if you seek help.

Emergency Services—Police, Fire, Ambulance
　　Call 000

Beyond Blue
　　https://www.beyondblue.org.au/

headspace
　　https://headspace.org.au/eheadspace/

Kids Helpline
　　https://kidshelpline.com.au/

Lifeline
　　https://www.lifeline.org.au/

Road Trauma Support Services
　　https://rtssv.org.au/

Traffic Accident Commission (TAC) Victoria
　　https://www.tac.vic.gov.au/

Words Carmen wrote in her get-well card to John after his accident.

Dad,
I love you,
I love you more than anything,
The feeling of darkness,
The feeling of loneliness,
The feeling of not having a farther
Nearly broke my heart,
The feeling of not seeing you,
Was like a bomb going off inside of me,
The thought,
The pain, that went through us all,
Was like a nothing,
A nothing that swept our hearts,
A nothing that dug deeper and deeper
every minute, every second of the day,
But then to hear your voice,
And to see your face,
It gave me that love,
That love that everyone of us
thought we had lost
I love you dad,
I love you more than anything
Love Carmen.c

www.ingramcontent.com/pod-product-compliance
Lightning Source LLC
Chambersburg PA
CBHW050314010526
44107CB00055B/2233